Sixties Style

Sixties Style

JUDITH MILLER

LONDON, NEW YORK,
MUNICH, MELBOURNE, DELHI

A joint production from DK and THE PRICE GUIDE COMPANY

DK DELHI
Designer Arunesh Talapatra
Editors Larissa Sayers, Aekta Jerath
Cutouts Neeraj Aggarwal
Managing Art Editor Aparna Sharma

DK LONDON
Editor Katie John   **Designer** Katie Eke
DTP, Reproduction, and Design Adam Walker
Production Elizabeth Warman
Managing Art Editor Heather McCarry

THE PRICE GUIDE COMPANY LIMITED
Publishing Manager Julie Brooke   **Editor** Jessica Bishop
Editorial Assistants Dan Dunlavey and Sandra Lange
Digital Image Co-ordinator Ellen Sinclair

While every care has been taken in the compilation of this guide, neither the authors nor the publishers accept any liability for any financial or other loss incurred by reliance placed on the information contained in *Sixties Style*.

First published in the USA in 2006 by DK Publishing, Inc.
375 Hudson Street, New York, NY 10014

First published in Great Britain in 2006 by Dorling Kindersley Limited,
80 Strand, London WC2R 0RL
A Penguin Company

The Price Guide Company (UK) Ltd: info@thepriceguidecompany.com

2 4 6 8 10 9 7 5 3 1

CIP catalog records for this book are available from the Library of Congress and the British Library.

UK ISBN-13: 978 1 4053 0628 7
UK ISBN-10: 1 4053 0628 9

US ISBN-13: 978-0-7566-1919-0
US ISBN-10: 0-7566-1919-X

Proofing by MDP, UK
Printed in China by Hung Hing Offset Printing Company Ltd

Discover more at
www.dk.com

CONTENTS

INTRODUCTION

Kicking off with The Beatles' residency at the Kaiser Keller in Hamburg and drawing to a close with Neil Armstrong's moonwalk, the 1960s was surely the most eventful decade in living memory. Revolutions in music, fashion, and public opinion rocked the fabric of society and are still being felt today. You might remember some of your worst excesses with a cringe, but I can guarantee that someone somewhere will still think your bell-bottomed pants are fabulous. For every collector who concentrates on a specific area, such as clothing or music, there are many more looking to add a touch of 1960s psychedelia to their homes. Bright colors and garish designs may not be the height of fashion today, but they still have the power to convey a sense of fun and freedom and keep the market in objects from the flower power era alive and well.

Judith Miller

Star Ratings

Each of the items in this book has a star rating according to its value:

★ under $100; under £50 ★★ $100–500; £50–200 ★★★ $500–800; £200–500

★★★★ $800–2,000; £500–1,000 ★★★★★ $2,000 upward; £1,000 upward

hot
pots

CERAMICS

Ceramic manufacturers in the 1960s embraced modernity and encouraged the fashionable principles of freedom of expression. As American ceramicist Robert Arneson stated, it seemed that there were "no worshipful old timers whose word was law ... everybody worked as they saw fit." The result was new, exciting ideas in terms of form and decoration.

Fiesta, Midwinter, Poole, and Troika were 1960s ceramic giants, and the vast diversity of their output reflects the revolutionary spirit of the time. Hand-thrown studio ware with abstract patterns and brown glazes was snapped up as quickly as simple black and white striped designs in new functional, cylindrical shapes. As well as being attractive, objects had to remain functional. Oven-to-table ware was particularly popular, as it appealed to busy modern women looking for a less formal approach to family mealtimes.

CERAMICS

Elizabethan English bone china "Pop" pattern mug and saucer; shape designed by A. Kusmirek. ★ ☆☆☆☆

English Ironstone Tableware "Flower Power" plate, by Washington Potteries, Staffordshire, England. ★ ☆ ☆ ☆

English Ironstone Tableware "Flower Power" teacup and saucer, by Washington Potteries, Staffordshire, England. ★ ☆ ☆ ☆

Rorstand "Florita" square dish. ★☆☆☆☆

Stig Lindberg for Gustavberg "Bersa" range, high-fired earthenware bowl, transfer-printed with geometric leaf design. ★☆☆☆☆

Langley teapot, with hand-painted
"Jamaica" or "Caribbean" design of
stylized vegetables. ★ ☆ ☆ ☆

Lord Nelson Pottery caster sugar
storage jar. ★ ☆ ☆ ☆

"Who ever said that pleasure wasn't functional?"

CHARLES EAMES, DESIGNER

DESIGNER PIECES

Lord Nelson Pottery "Gaytime" butter dish.

☆☆☆☆
★

Buchan Pottery hand-painted tankard in "Riviera" pattern; designer unknown. ★ ☆☆☆☆

Hornsea Pottery mug, designed by John Clappison, decorated with stylized design of a train and coaches. *1967* ★ ☆☆☆☆

Wedgwood "Blue Anemone" pattern cup and saucer, designed by Susie Cooper, with printed marks. ★ ☆ ☆ ☆

Small square plate by Surrey Ceramics, with abstract floral design and impressed marks. ★ ☆ ☆ ☆

CERAMICS

Midwinter Pottery "Mosaic" pattern
hors d'oeuvres dish, designed by
Jessie Tait. *1960* ★★☆☆☆

MIDWINTER

Britain was thirsty for exciting, new ideas after the restrictions of the Second World War, and the world of ceramics was no exception. The Staffordshire-based Midwinter Pottery was particularly quick to recognize the demand for fashionable ceramics, and began to reject traditional styles in favor of the modern shapes popular with US designers. The designer Jessie Tait (b.1928) contributed to Midwinter's postwar success. Her innovative designs, including the well-known Primavera, Fiesta, and Zambesi ranges, are very popular with collectors today.

Abstract patterns and highly stylized floral, fruit, or foliate designs are typical of Midwinter's 1960s products, and contemporary textiles were often an inspiration. Patterns that sum up the style and feeling of the time are particularly desirable today, as are characteristic pieces that combine such patterns with a typically modern shape.

DETAIL: Mark giving names of artist and pattern.

CERAMICS

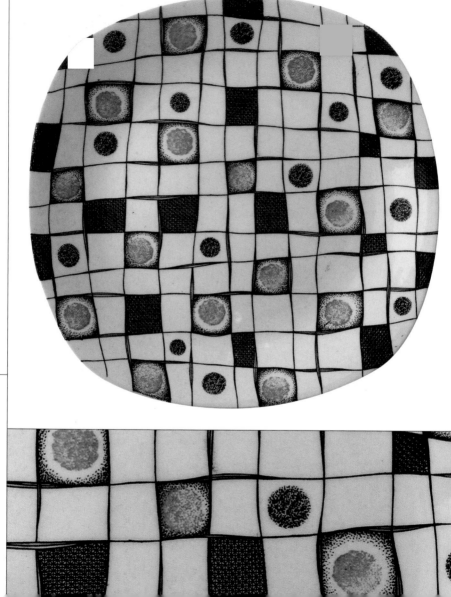

Midwinter Pottery plate in "Homespun" pattern, designed by Jessie Tait. ★★☆☆☆

Midwinter Pottery "Sienna" pattern transfer-printed plate, by Jessie Tait; one of the most popular designs from the Fine range, launched in 1962. ★ ☆ ☆ ☆ ☆

Midwinter Pottery trio in "Fashion" shape,
with hand-painted "Border Stripe" pattern,
designed by Jessie Tait. *1960* ★☆☆☆☆

Midwinter Pottery "Tango" pattern coffee-pot, designed by Eve Midwinter. ★☆☆☆☆

Midwinter Pottery "Fine" coffee set, with transfer-printed "Cherry Tree" pattern; designed by Nigel Wylde. *1966* ★ ☆ ☆ ☆

J. and G. Meakin Studio coffee service in "Cornflower" pattern. ★ ☆ ☆ ☆

PORTMEIRION

Susan Williams-Ellis and her husband bought the famous Gray's Pottery of Stoke-on-Trent, England, in 1960. The company concentrated on the production of decorative items to sell in its gift shop in the Welsh village of Portmeirion, which had been created by Susan's father, Sir Clough Williams-Ellis, in 1925.

Susan started to design patterns and later shapes for the company. The simplicity of her forms made them immediately popular, and soon Portmeirion was struggling to keep up with demand. Her designs tend to have clean-lines and cylindrical shapes, allowing the easiest and best display of transfers. The "Greek Key" pattern was one of the first designs to appear on her tall, cylindrical coffee sets, in the early 1960s. Her "Totem" design, launched in 1963, earned Portmeirion a reputation for innovation. Another pattern, "Talisman," comprises two strong, abstract black shapes over-printed with blocks of color, with gaps to hide failure of register or breaks in the print.

Two Portmeirion Potteries "Greek Key" pattern coffee pots, designed by Susan Williams-Ellis. *1968* ★ ☆ ☆ ☆ ☆

PORTMEIRION

Portmeirion Potteries Seraph coffee set in "Tivoli" pattern, designed by Susan Williams-Ellis; comprises six cups with saucers, jug, and coffee-pot.   *c.1964*   ★★★ ☆☆

Portmeirion Potteries "Jupiter" pattern coffee-pot, designed by Susan Williams-Ellis, with printed marks. ★ ★ ☆ ☆ ☆

English coffee-pot, with impressed mark "Price Made in England." ★ ☆☆☆☆

Portmeirion Potteries "Talisman" pattern
vegetable dish, designed by Susan
Williams-Ellis. c.1962
★★★☆☆

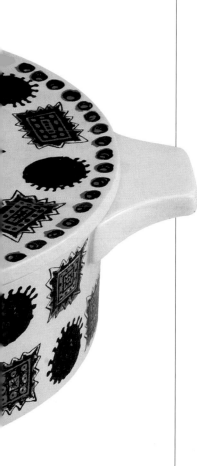

Portmeirion Potteries "Monte Sol" pattern
transfer-printed storage jar, designed by Susan
Williams-Ellis. *1966* ★ ☆☆☆

Portmeirion Potteries 'Dolphin" pattern tea storage jar, by Susan Williams-Ellis, with printed marks. ★★☆☆☆

Set of three Portmeirion Potteries storage jars, with transfer-printed "Talisman" pattern, by Susan Williams-Ellis. *c.1962* ★★☆☆☆

Pair of Carlton Ware salt and pepper shakers, shaped as an "Arabian" king and queen. ★ ☆☆☆☆

Staffordshire Potteries storage jar, with plastic faux wood lid; transfer-printed with psychedelic flower pattern. ★ ☆☆☆☆

Poole Pottery "Delphis" plate, painted by Susan Allen, in abstract floral design. ★ ☆☆☆☆

POOLE POTTERY

The company now known as Poole Pottery originated in 1921 as Carter, Stabler and Adams, a subsidiary of Carter Pottery, established to produce decorative ceramics. The firm's various incarnations, based in Poole, England, set new trends throughout the 20th century.

During the 1920s and 1930s, the company produced vases, plates, jugs, and other wares, which were painted with bold, abstract patterns by a team of artists. Famous designs included "Studland," with its angular handles, and the floral "Picotee."

The "Delphis Collection" of hand-made and hand-decorated pieces was launched by Poole Pottery in 1963. Pieces featured bright natural or abstract designs in oranges, yellows, and browns, in keeping with the fashions of the decade. The ethnic and organic shapes and vibrant hues were also distinctively 1960s. Designs involving bold stripes, wavy lines, and branches, inspired by Swedish ceramics, were particularly popular. This combination of up-to-date design and traditional skills has made Poole pottery highly collectible today.

Poole Pottery "Delphis" plate, with red and orange starburst design painted by Susan Allen.
★★☆☆☆

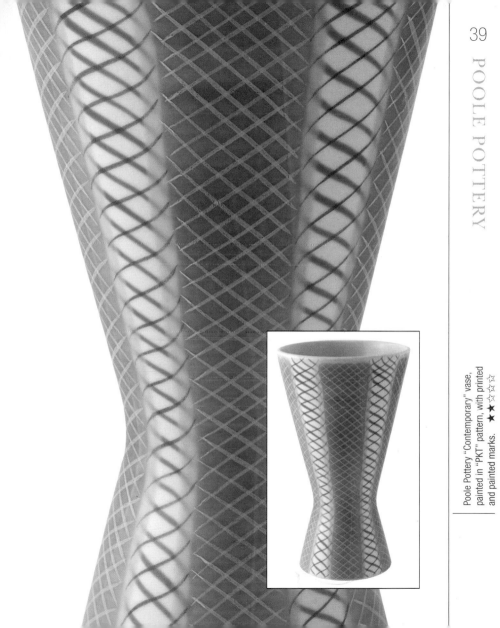

Poole Pottery "Contemporary" vase, painted in "PKT" pattern, with printed and painted marks. ★ ★ ☆ ☆ ☆

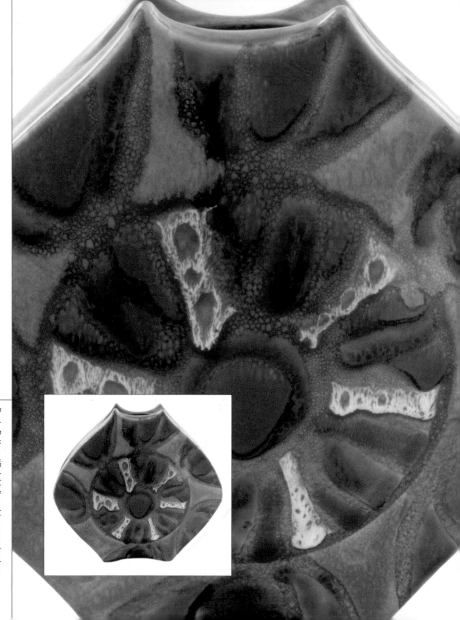

Poole Pottery "Delphis" cushion vase in shape 90, with abstract wheel design possibly by Shirley Campbell. 1967 ★★☆☆☆

Poole Pottery "Delphis" vase, with factory and painter's marks to base. ★ ☆☆☆

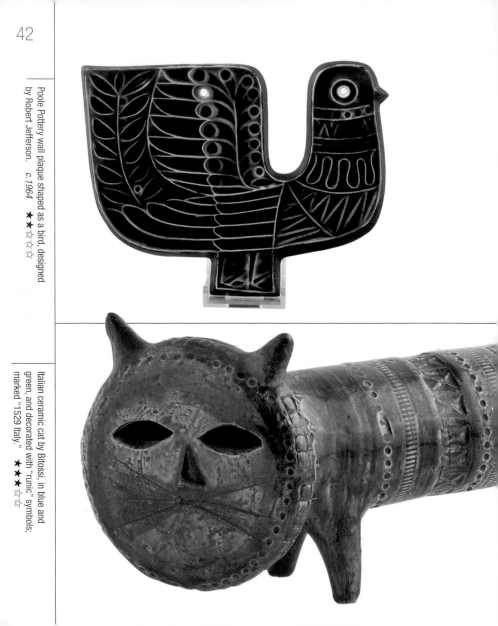

Poole Pottery wall plaque shaped as a bird, designed by Robert Jefferson. *c.1964* ★★☆☆☆

Italian ceramic cat by Bitossi, in blue and green, and decorated with "runic" symbols; marked "1529 Italy." ★★★☆☆

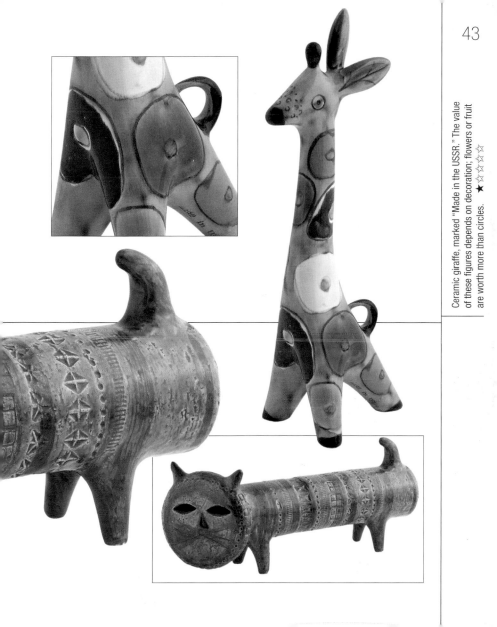

Ceramic giraffe, marked "Made in the USSR." The value of these figures depends on decoration; flowers or fruit are worth more than circles. ★ ☆ ☆ ☆ ☆

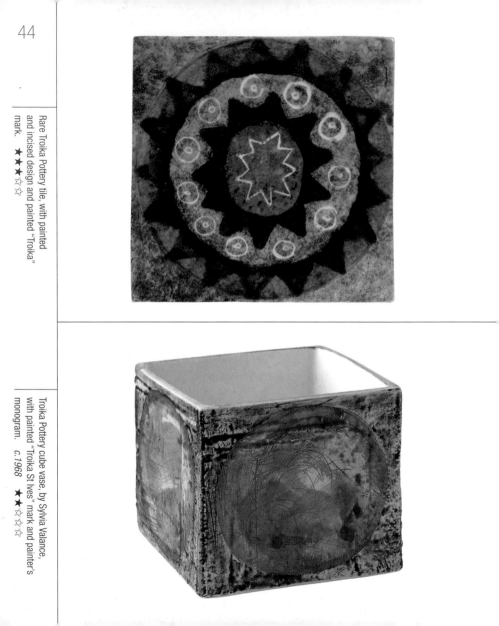

Rare Troika Pottery tile, with painted and incised design and painted "Troika" mark. ★★★☆☆

Troika Pottery cube vase, by Sylvia Valance, with painted "Troika St Ives" mark and painter's monogram. *c.1968* ★★☆☆☆

Troika Pottery cylinder vase, with painted mark "Troika St Ives England" and artist's monogram. ★★☆☆☆

FIESTA

Generations of Americans have adored the cheerful look of Fiesta Ware, produced by the Homer Laughlin China Company of Newell, West Virginia. The range was created by noted ceramicist Frederick Rhead (1880–1942), who had joined the company in 1927, and the first pieces were released in 1936.

Simple, bright finishes met the public demand for colorful objects for the home, and by limiting glazes to single tones and creating streamlined pieces, the company came up with a product that was very much of its age – modern, striking, and highly desirable. The manufacture of "vintage" Fiesta slowed in 1969 and was finally ended in 1973, but modern pieces are still produced today. The value of Fiesta pieces depends on their color and shape. Although the styling of the pitcher shown here is influenced by the Art Deco Movement, the bright yellow color and striking shape are typical of the 1960s. The concentric rings echo popular psychedelic circle designs of the period.

CERAMICS

Small Fiesta bowl with lid, in red. ★★★☆☆

Fiesta bowl, in forest green. ★★☆☆☆

★★☆☆

Fiesta teapot, in turquoise.

"Tiki" mug, shaped as an Easter Island head, marked "Japan." ★ ☆☆☆☆

★★★ ☆☆

Sylvac, Lemon "face" pot, stamped, "4895." "3695."

SylvaC "Uncle Sam" character jug, stamped "2888." ★★☆☆☆

Enesco "Jackie Kennedy Onassis In Mourning" lady head vase, commemorating the shooting of John F. Kennedy. *c.1963* ★★★☆☆

SylvaC "John F. Kennedy" character jug, stamps, "2689," "2682." ☆☆☆ ★★

Granforest hand-painted ceramic cookie jar, with handle. ★ ☆ ☆ ☆ ☆

★ ★ ★ ☆ ☆

"Howdy Doody," Purinton cookie jar.

p.257

p.52

p.338

p.355

p.422

p.323

p.339

p.378

p.392

p.361

p.337

p.336　　　　　　　　　　p.347　　　　　　　　　p.320

p.55　　　　　　　　　　p.329　　　　　　　　　p.421

p.52　　　　　　　　　　p.52　　　　　　　　　p.145

AMERICANA

Swedish biscuit barrel, with wooden lid,
labeled "Gogay tableware;" has impressed
marks and numbers.
★ ☆ ☆ ☆ ☆

Set of four Staffordshire Potteries stacking mugs, printed with cartoons of fashionable people. ★ ☆☆☆

Burleigh dish with "Orbit" pattern, a psychedelic "Op Art" design. ★☆☆☆☆

Set of three Pyrosil casserole dishes. ★☆☆☆☆

Johnson Bros. coffee-pot, in a variation of "Focus" pattern designed by Barbara Brown for Midwinter Pottery. *1964* ★ ☆☆☆

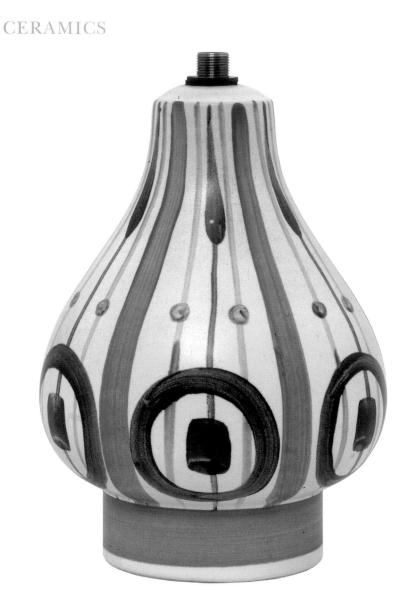

Glyn Colledge lamp base for Langley Pottery, hand-painted with orange stripes and brown circles. ★★☆☆☆

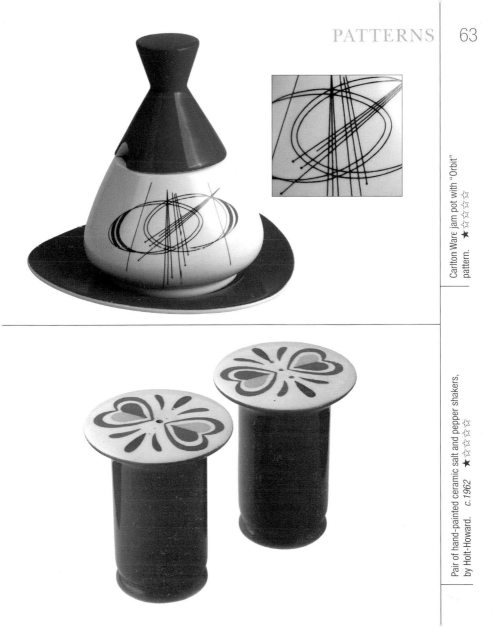

Carlton Ware jam pot with "Orbit" pattern. ★ ☆☆☆

Pair of hand-painted ceramic salt and pepper shakers, by Holt-Howard. c.1962 ★ ☆☆☆

Denby hand-painted coffee-pot in "Arabesque" pattern, designed by Gill Pemberton. This pattern was known as "Samarkand" in the US. ★☆☆☆☆

Waisted Iden Pottery vase, glazed with wax-resist technique;
has printed mark to base. *1965* ★ ☆ ☆ ☆

Cornishware cafetière, made for the
Australian market. ★★☆☆☆

Kupittaan Savi studio vase, with stylized vine decoration on blue ground; marked "Kupittaan Finland." ★★★☆☆

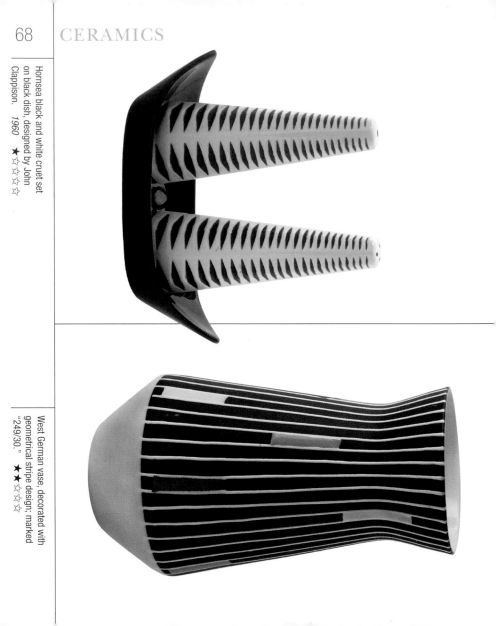

Hornsea black and white cruet set on black dish, designed by John Clappison. *1960* ★ ☆ ☆ ☆ ☆

West German vase, decorated with geometrical stripe design; marked "249/30." ★ ★ ☆ ☆ ☆

Tall slipware vase by Hornsea Pottery; base is stamped
with mold number "85." *1963*

★ ☆ ☆
★ ☆

CERAMICS

"*The details are not the details. They make the design.*"

CHARLES EAMES, DESIGNER

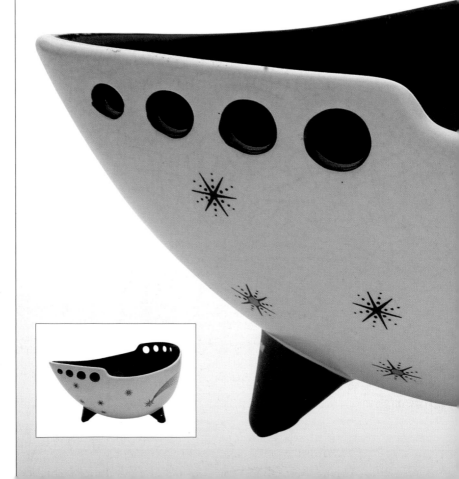

Wade Pottery "Harmony" vase, with "Shooting Stars" pattern. ★★☆☆

Beswick vase designed by Albert Hallam, with "Zebra" pattern; marked "1351." ★★☆☆☆

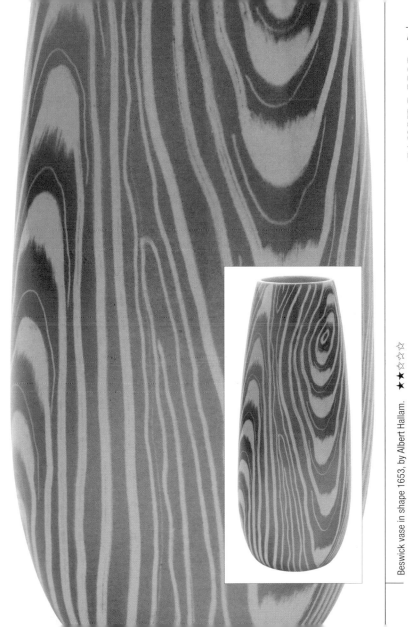

PATTERNS

★★☆☆

Beswick vase in shape 1653, by Albert Hallam.

Set of 3 Beer Goblets (not illustrated)—14/6.
Glasses also available without decoration

'SLIM JIMS' matching sets of

Sh

Sherdley glass

'CHUBBIES' matchin

tumblers in various

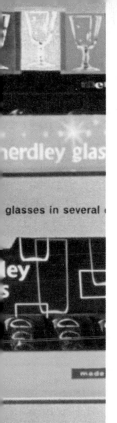

GLASSWARE

While exciting new plastic objects were hugely in demand, glass was also enjoying a revival. Funky forms, textured surfaces, and bold colors replaced traditional forms and decoration.

Some of the most stylish and innovative glass of the 1960s came from Italy and Scandinavia. Italian glassmakers typically produced thick-walled, sophisticated, and sometimes witty, shapes with an exuberance of color, designed to complement stylish interiors of the period. The textured forms of Finnish designer Timo Sarpaneva reflected the mood for experimentation. Blenko in the US concentrated on sculptural shapes, while in Britain, radical shapes and bright psychedelic colors helped put Whitefriars glassworks on the post-war style map.  Geoffrey Baxter's range of textured vases – which included the now highly sought-after "Drunken Bricklayer" and "Banjo" vases – contributed to the company's success during the period.

Blenko amberina vase; model number 6223.   *c.1962*   ★★☆☆☆

Blenko "Olive Green" daisy vase, designed by Wayne Husted; design number 6115L. ☆☆☆ ★★

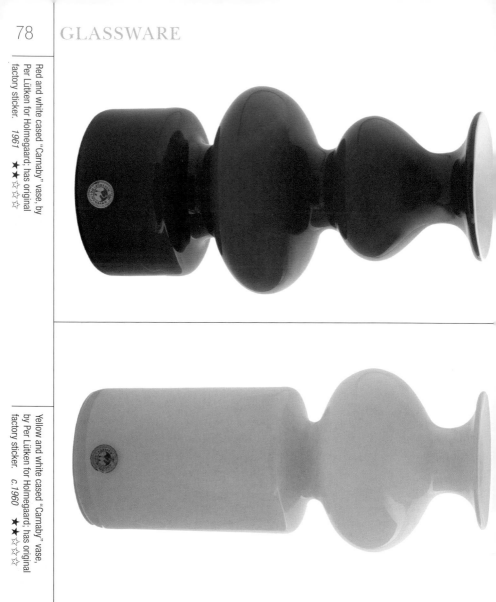

Red and white cased "Carnaby" vase, by Per Lütken for Holmegaard; has original factory sticker. *1961* ★★☆☆☆

Yellow and white cased "Carnaby" vase, by Per Lütken for Holmegaard; has original factory sticker. *c.1960* ★★☆☆☆

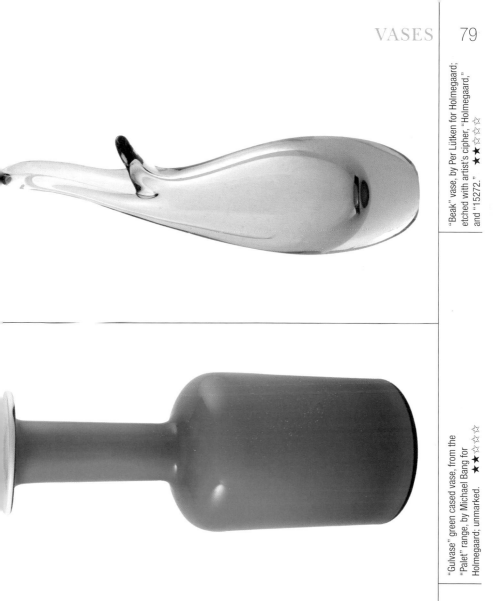

"Gulvase" green cased vase, from the "Palet" range, by Michael Bang for Holmegaard; unmarked. ★ ★ ☆ ☆ ☆

"Beak" vase, by Per Lütken for Holmegaard; etched with artist's cipher, "Holmegaard," and "15272." ★ ★ ☆ ☆ ☆

Vase designed by Flavio Poli, by Seguso Vetri d'Arte, in purple and yellow cased glass.

★★☆☆☆

Vase designed by Flavio Poli, by Seguso Vetri d'Arte, in green and purple cased glass. *c.1960* ★★★★

Murano cased glass vase – made using the *sommerso* technique – showing characteristic "halo" effect in interior. ★★ ☆☆☆

Venini and Co. "Pezzato" vase, designed by Fulvio Bianconi, decorated with colored plates of melted glass; marked "venini ITALY murano" on base. ★★★★★

Fratelli Toso "Kiku" vase, designed by Ermanno Toso, in clear glass with murrines in floral shapes. *c.1960* ★★★★

WHITEFRIARS

The Whitefriars glassworks was one of the oldest and most eminent glassmakers in Britain. Whitefriars' designer Geoffrey Baxter was a leading figure in postwar British glass design. After working on a number of successful designs, Baxter launched his innovative "Textured" range in 1967, which is extremely popular with collectors today. He made the original textured molds in his spare time, from objects that he chanced on, including tree bark and nails. The internal protrusions caused by these objects created interesting surface effects. The avant-garde shapes and outlandish psychedelic colors, such as tangerine orange and kingfisher blue, helped increase sales.

The "Drunken Bricklayer" vase, one of Baxter's most characteristic designs, shows his interest in looking to the world around him for inspiration. For this piece, man-made objects such as piled bricks inspired him rather more than natural textures and forms.

Whitefriars "Drunken Bricklayer" vase in kingfisher blue, by Geoffrey Baxter; pattern number 9672. ★★★★

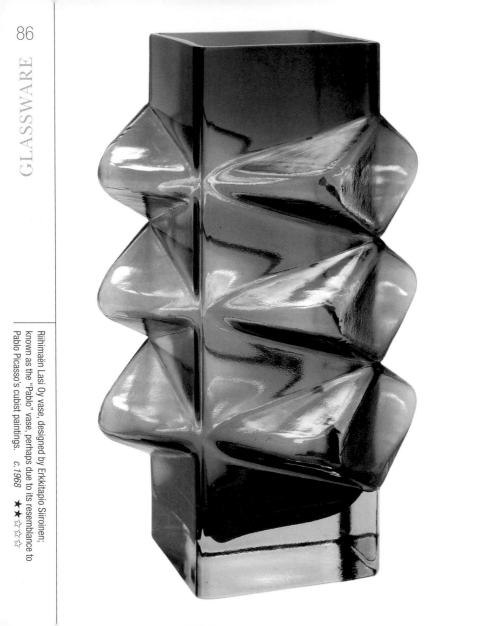

Riihimaën Lasi Oy vase, designed by Erkkitapio Siiroinen; known as the "Pablo" vase, perhaps due to its resemblance to Pablo Picasso's cubist paintings.   *c.1968*   ★★☆☆☆

Riihimaën Lasi Oy green geometric
"Disc" vase, designed by Tamara
Aladin. ★ ★ ☆ ☆

Riihimaën Lasi Oy red glass
vase, designed by Tamara
Aladin. *1965* ★ ☆ ☆ ☆

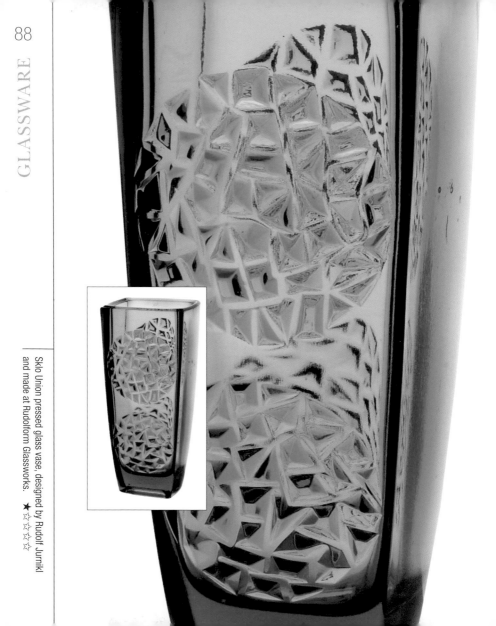

Sklo Union pressed glass vase, designed by Rudolf Jurniki and made at Rudolfform Glassworks. ★ ☆ ☆ ☆ ☆

★ ☆☆ ☆☆

Sklo Union pressed glass vase, designed by
Vladislav Urba and made at Rosice Glassworks.

Whitefriars Kingfisher blue "Banjo" vase, designed by Geoffrey Baxter, with molded abstract design on sides. ★★★★★

Whitefriars orange TV vase, designed by Geoffrey Baxter. *c.1967* ★★☆☆☆

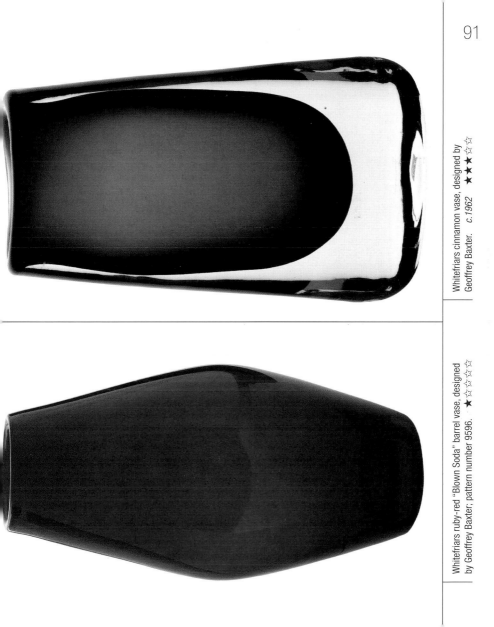

Whitefriars cinnamon vase, designed by
Geoffrey Baxter.   *c.1962*   ★ ★ ★ ☆

Whitefriars ruby-red "Blown Soda" barrel vase, designed
by Geoffrey Baxter; pattern number 9596.   ★ ☆ ☆ ☆

Ball-shaped vase, by Glasfabriek Leerdam, with orange color graduating into red. *c.1965* ★★☆☆☆

Pair of early Dartington "Greek Key" vases, in orange glass, designed by Frank Thrower. ★ ★ ☆ ☆ ☆

Chance "Aqualux" handkerchief vase, in brown hammered glass. ★ ☆ ☆ ☆

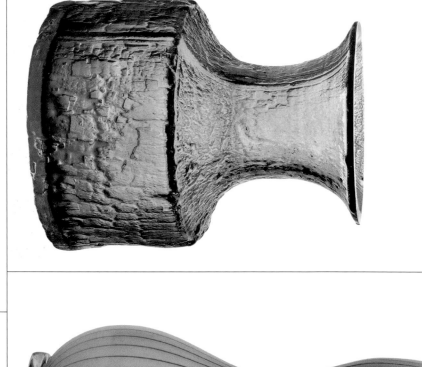

Iittala bark-patterned "Finlandia" vase, designed by Timo Sarpaneva; signed "TIMO SARPANEVA 3331" on base.   c.1964   ★★☆☆☆

Vicke Lindstrand "Unica" vase, designed by Kosta, in cream glass with red strands.   c.1960   ★★★☆☆

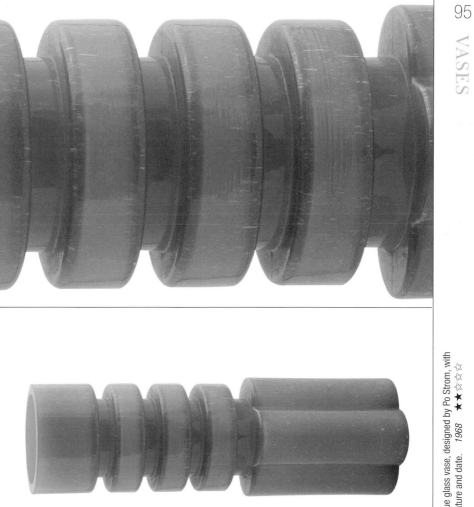

Alsterfors blue glass vase, designed by Po Strom, with
etched signature and date. *1968* ★ ★ ☆ ☆ ☆

p.90

p.247

p.218

p.92

p.61

p.138

p.128

p.173

p.431

p.76

p.262

p.41

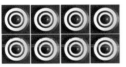

p.249

p.152

p.439

p.219

p.137

p.238

Mdina "Fish" vase, cased in clear glass, designed and made by Michael Harris. ★★★☆☆

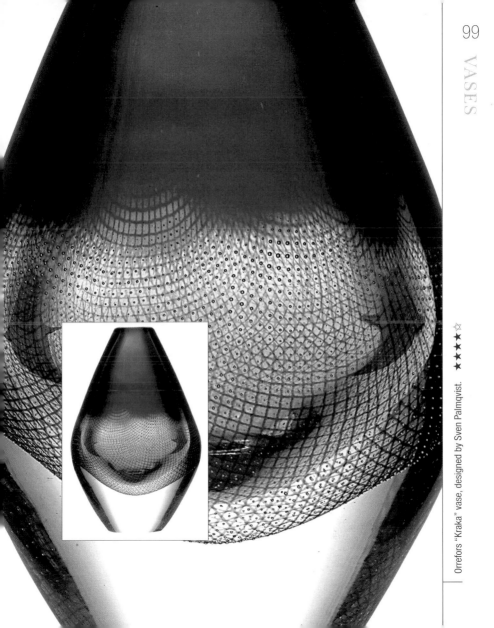

★★★☆

Orrefors "Kraka" vase, designed by Sven Palmqvist.

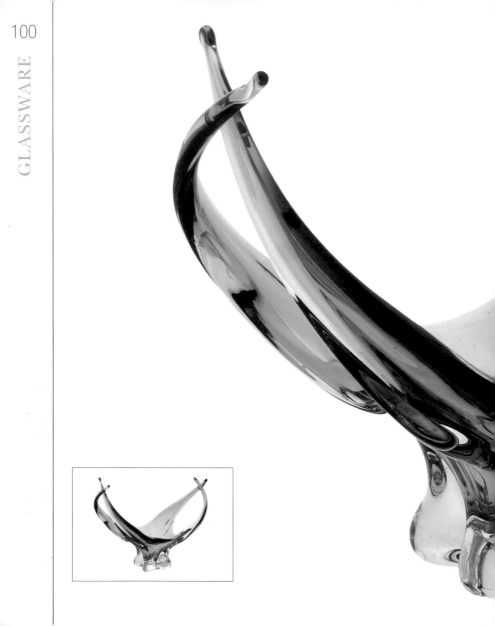

Decorative art glass such as this bowl was popular between the 1950s and the 1970s and was widely sold in department stores.

Canadian blue and clear glass "Chalet" glass bowl, with acid-etched mark on base. ★ ☆ ☆ ☆ ☆

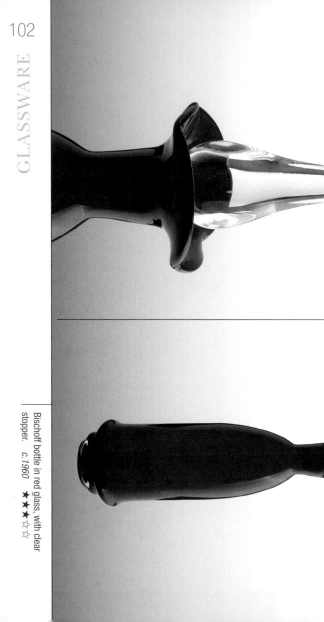

Bischoff bottle in red glass, with clear stopper. *c.1960* ★★★ ☆☆

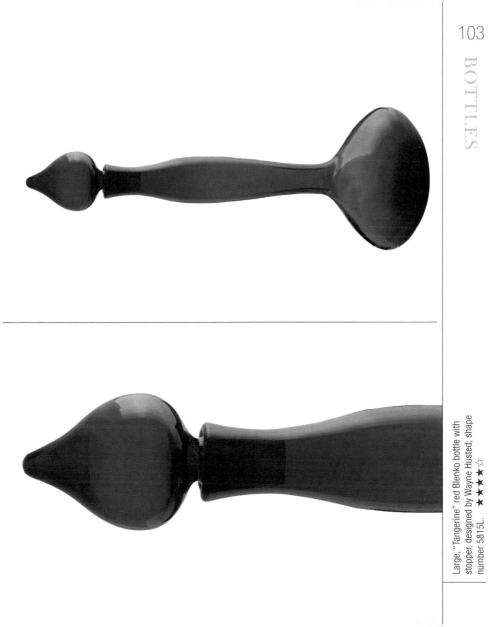

Large, "Tangerine" red Blenko bottle with stopper, designed by Wayne Husted; shape number 5815L. ★★★★ ☆

GLASSWARE

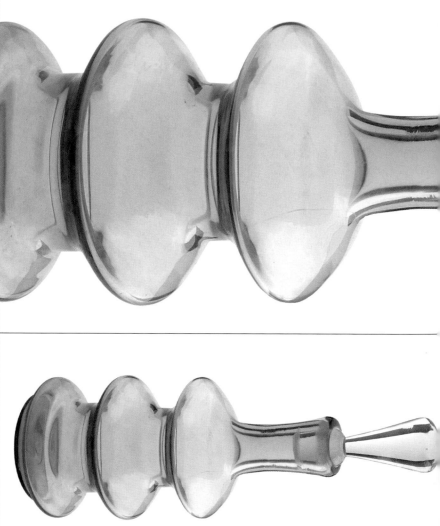

Bischoff bottle in pale yellow glass, with clear stopper. *c.1960*   ★★☆☆☆

Blenko "Jonquil" yellow bottle, with stopper, by Joe Philip Myers; design number 649. ★★☆☆ ★★★

WEDGWOOD

The name "Wedgwood" was given to the products of the King's Lynn Glass factory, based in Norfolk, England, when the Wedgwood Group took it over in 1969. The factory had been founded two years earlier by the eminent glassware designer Ronald Stennett-Willson, and specialized in producing high-quality decorative items and tableware in the popular Scandinavian style. Wedgwood forms were clean and modern, relying on the color and clarity of the glass. Colors tended to be either coolly classical or strong and striking.

The "Sheringham" candlestick was designed in various sizes, with one, two, three, five, seven, and nine disks, and was available in seven colors. These multidisk candlesticks were particularly difficult to make, and received considerable public attention and critical acclaim. Collectors today usually pay higher prices for candlesticks with larger numbers of disks.

"Sheringham" candlesticks, designed by Ronald Stennett-Willson for Kings Lynn Glass (prior to its takeover by Wedgwood). *1967* ★ ★ ★ ★ ★

"Carnaby" candlesticks, by Per Lütken for Holmegaard; one candlestick has original paper label. ★★☆☆☆

"Brancaster" candlesticks, by Ronald Stennett-Wilson for Wedgwood. *1967* ★★★ ☆☆

Lime-green milk glass "Gin" decanter, with stopper made from turned, painted wood. ★ ☆☆☆☆☆

Tomato-red milk glass "Whisky" decanter, with stopper made from turned, painted wood. ★ ☆☆☆☆

Ravenhead "Slim Jim" drinking glass in "Royalty" pattern, by Alexander Hardie Williamson. *c.1964* ★ ☆ ☆ ☆ ☆

★ ☆☆☆☆ Screen-printed "LOVE" drinking glass.

Gold-rimmed Ravenhead drinking glass in "Gaytime" pattern, by Alexander Hardie Williamson. ★☆☆☆☆

Ravenhead tumbler in "Maple" pattern, by Alexander Hardie Williamson. ★☆☆☆☆

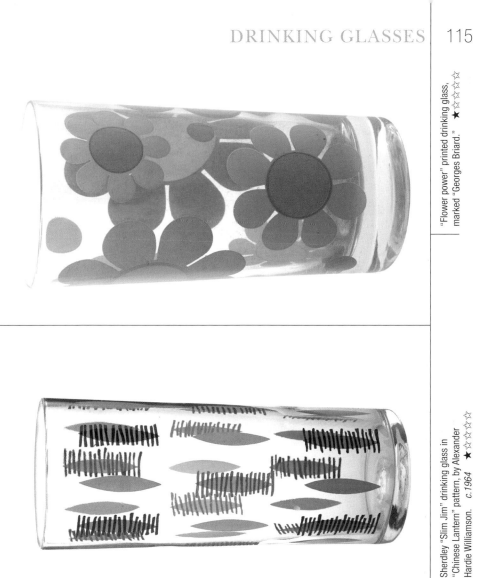

"Flower power" printed drinking glass, marked "Georges Briard." ★ ☆☆☆

Sherdley "Slim Jim" drinking glass in "Chinese Lantern" pattern, by Alexander Hardie Williamson. *c.1964* ★ ☆☆☆

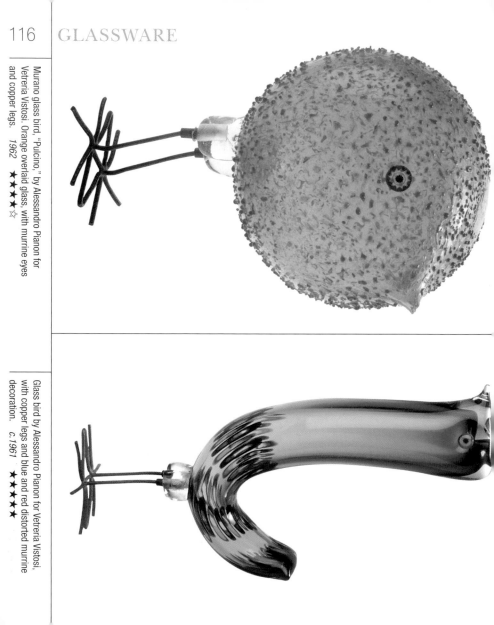

Murano glass bird, "Pulcino," by Alessandro Pianon for Vetreria Vistosi. Orange overlaid glass, with murrine eyes and copper legs. *1962* ★★★★☆

Glass bird by Alessandro Pianon for Vetreria Vistosi, with copper legs and blue and red distorted murrine decoration. *c.1961* ★★★★★

ORNAMENTAL GLASS

Caithness Glass lamp base, in purple glass,
designed by Domhnall O'Broin; has original
factory label.   *c.1967*   ★ ★   ☆ ☆ ☆

PETER MAX

By combining stylized comic strip graphics with undulating lines and psychedelic colors, Peter Max produced some of the most striking and influential art of the 1960s. Max was born in Berlin, Germany, in 1937, and his family settled in the US in 1953. He went on to study at the Arts Student League in Manhattan, and began experimenting with photomontage and colorful silkscreens in the 1960s.

Max's "cosmic" style, typified by chunky line drawings filled with blocks of color, was a huge commercial success, appearing on everything from pencil cases to music posters. The far-out imagery of skyscapes, sunbursts, and clouds, inspired by his childhood in China and trips to India, Africa, and Israel, appealed to a generation that was open to experimenting with mystical cultures and mind-altering drugs. Peter Max has subsequently designed postage stamps for the United Nations and painted commissioned work for five US Presidents, including Ronald Reagan and Bill Clinton.

☆☆☆
★★★

Peter Max glass dish, with characteristic flower decoration at center.

"Style is primarily a matter of instinct."

BILL BLASS, DESIGNER

☆☆☆
★★★

Large Murano glass lamp, attributed to
Cenendese.   *c.1960*

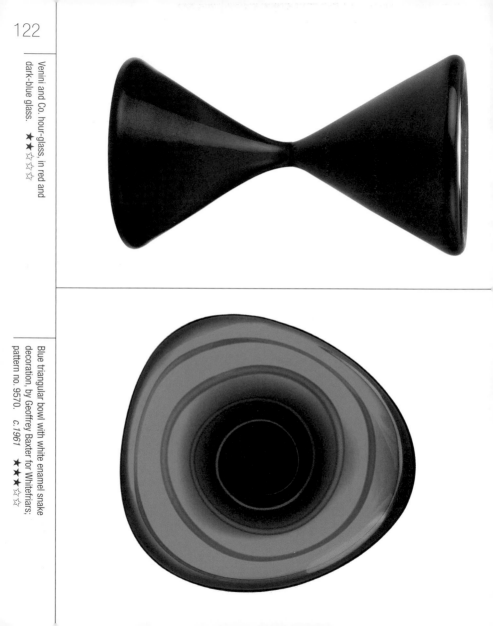

Venini and Co. hour-glass, in red and dark-blue glass. ★★☆☆☆

Blue triangular bowl with white enamel snake decoration, by Geoffrey Baxter for Whitefriars; pattern no. 9570. c.1961 ★★★☆☆

Fiestaware fluted plate by Chance, with floral decoration. ★ ☆☆☆☆

FLOWER POWER

p.115

p.119

p.175

p.276

p.258

p.136

p.36

p.283

p.11

p.260

p.135

p.318

p.174

p.11

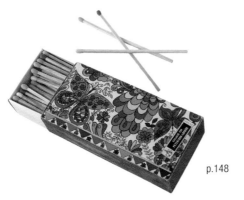

p.148

p.122

FLOWER POWER

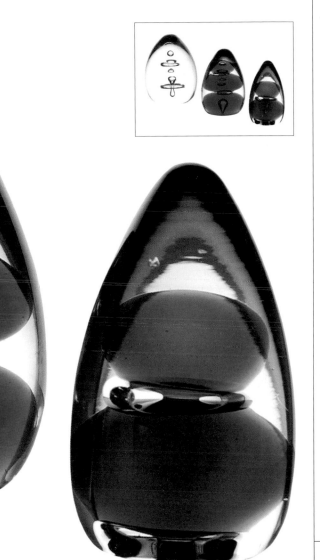

☆☆☆ ★★

Paperweights by Ronald Stennett-Willson, for
King's Lynn Glass. *1967*

GLASSWARE

Orange bowl by Higgins Glass Studio. ★★☆☆☆

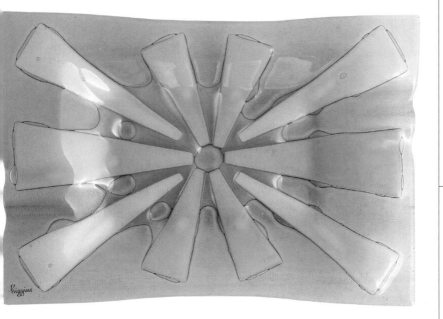

Rectangular green dish by Higgins Glass Studio. ★★☆☆

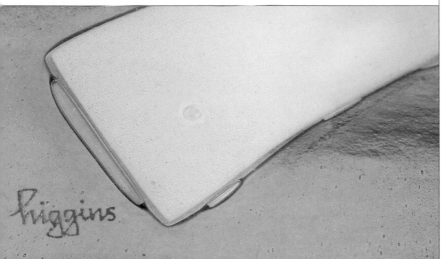

DETAIL: Maker's signature at corner.

HOMEWARE

As well as expressing themselves through dress sense, Sixties followers of fashion aspired to trendy homes full of the latest designer furniture and nifty gadgets. The question of whether to own a television, record player, or telephone had evolved into decisions over which brand, model, and color to choose. Almost everything, from coat hangers to teacups, was decorated with swirling flowers or Op Art patterns.

Design was no longer just about function, economy, and longevity, but increasingly embraced visual impact and stylishness. Manufacturers attempted to meet the higher expectations of a demanding public and their craving for novelty by churning out innovative designs. The archetypical material was plastic, typically in brightly colored psychedelic shades or cool space-age colors.

Old Hall stainless steel "Alveston" tea set, designed by Roberts Welch, comprising tea pot, hot water jug, milk jug, and sugar bowl. *c.1962* ★★★☆☆

Viners stainless steel and gold-plated wine goblet, designed by Stuart Devlin. ★☆☆☆☆

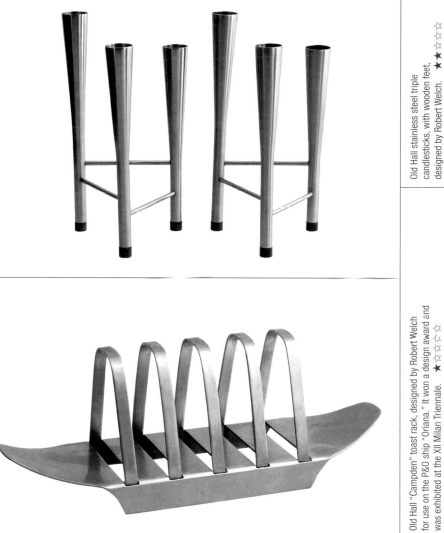

Old Hall stainless steel triple candlesticks, with wooden feet, designed by Robert Welch. ★ ☆ ☆ ☆

Old Hall "Campden" toast rack, designed by Robert Welch for use on the P&O ship "Oriana." It won a design award and was exhibited at the XII Milan Triennale. ★ ☆ ☆ ☆

Red enameled cooking pot with lid, and matching kettle. ★★☆☆☆

Norwegian enameled kettle with stylized leaf pattern in white. ★☆☆☆☆

Finel enameled metal saucepan with lid and vegetable design. ★ ☆ ☆ ☆

Saucepan with stylized floral design and blue lid. ★ ☆ ☆ ☆

"Flower power" bread board in melamine. ★☆☆☆☆

Orange tea cup and saucer in Melaware, by Ranton and Co. ★ ☆☆☆☆

Plastic condiment server, with pineapple-shaped salt shaker, grapefruit-shaped pepper shaker, and sugar bowl; base is marked "Starke Design, Inc., Bklyn, N.Y." ★ ☆☆☆☆

Plastic Fiesta snack set, made in Spain by Transplastic S.A., with four stacked, rotating bowls; has original box. ★ ☆☆☆☆

Braun coffee-grinder, designed
by Dieter Rams. ★ ☆ ☆ ☆

Cheeseboard and knife; board has inset tile panel with stylized floral design. ★☆☆☆☆

Metal-framed "flower power" trivet; has printed tile panel with "Peace" design. ★ ☆ ☆ ☆

Houze art glass ashtray from Vietnam War, with topical cartoon: "Get well soon – your doctor just got drafted." ★ ☆☆☆☆

Football Association "1966 World Cup Willie" ashtray, by Washington Pottery, Staffordshire; rare. *c.1966* ★★☆☆

Group of stacking ashtrays in molded plastic, marked "DO Reg No. 954.589 Pentagram." ★★☆☆☆

DETAIL: Stacked ashtrays with interlocked edges.

Iroquois China "Love" ashtray, designed by Peter Max. ★ ★ ☆ ☆ ☆

Ceramic ashtray commemorating John F. Kennedy's visit to Berlin. ★ ★ ☆ ☆ ☆

BACHELOR BOY

p.273

p.370

p.324

p.404

p.16

p.148

p.236

p.371

p.159

p.434

p.270

p.433

p.372

p.396

p.59

p.406

p.339

Zippo pocket cigarette lighter with Coca-Cola advertisement; has original box. *Early 1960s* ★★★☆

Box of matches, with psychedelic cover by Peter John. ★☆☆☆

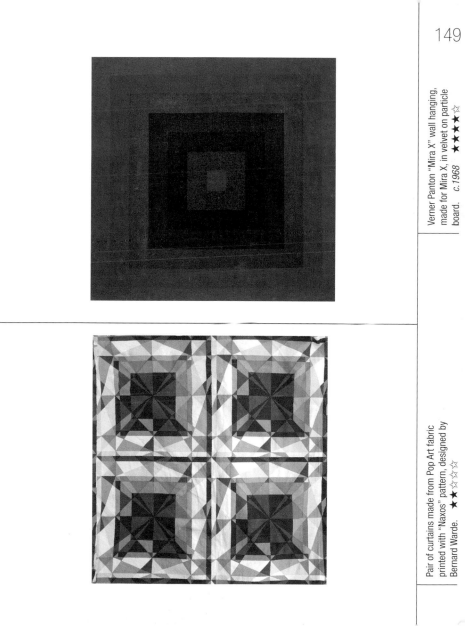

Verner Panton "Mira X" wall hanging, made for Mira X, in velvet on particle board. *c.1968* ★★★★☆

Pair of curtains made from Pop Art fabric printed with "Naxos" pattern, designed by Bernard Warde. ★★☆☆☆

Verner Panton "Marguerite" rug, by Unika Vaev,
Copenhagen, in wool, underlaid with upholstery
fabric. *c.1965* ★★★★★☆

Orange and pink string art picture of
butterfly. ★☆☆☆☆

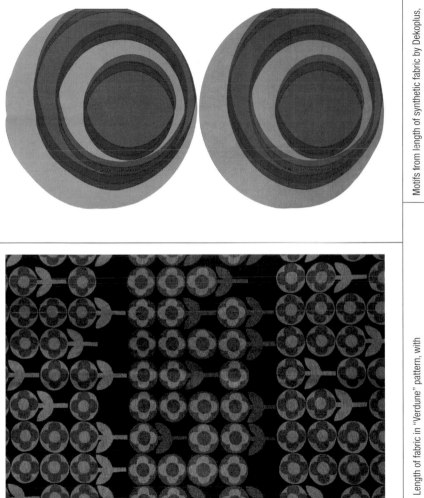

Motifs from length of synthetic fabric by Dekoplus, printed in shades of blue with design possibly by Pierre Cardin. ★ ☆☆☆

Length of fabric in "Verdune" pattern, with printed floral design on dark blue ground, by Peter Hall for Heals. ★ ☆☆☆

Length of fabric with psychedelic orange and yellow pattern. ★☆☆☆☆

inflatable plastic cushion by Peter Max, depicting a group of psychedelic heads. ★ ★ ☆ ☆

Inflatable plastic cushion by Peter Max, printed with smiling mouth, tulip borders, and the word "Hello." ★ ★ ☆ ☆ ☆

ERICOFON

The Swedish company L. M. Ericsson has been making telephones since the 19th century. Now largely associated with cellphone technology, in the mid-20th century it was renowned for producing the Ericofon – a small, lightweight phone that was easy to use.

The Ericofon was designed in the late 1940s and was first produced in 1954. It was made in a wide variety of colors that appealed to houseproud buyers keen on consumer choice. "Ericofon brings a fresh look to every room of the house," one advertisement claimed. The stylish one-piece design, incorporating a dial in the base of the phone, was an additional lure. During the 1960s, demand for the Ericofon was high, with US sales exceeding capacity by 500 percent. In 1967, Ericsson introduced the pushbutton Ericofon, with ten keys. Production was discontinued in 1972. Anyone wishing to collect these telephones should be aware that reproductions are now on the market.

Cream-colored plastic Ericofon telephone, by Ericsson. ★★☆☆

"We become what we behold. We shape our tools and then our tools shape us."

MARSHALL McLUHAN, SOCIOLOGIST

Red plastic telephone by the Reliance Telephone Company. ★★☆☆

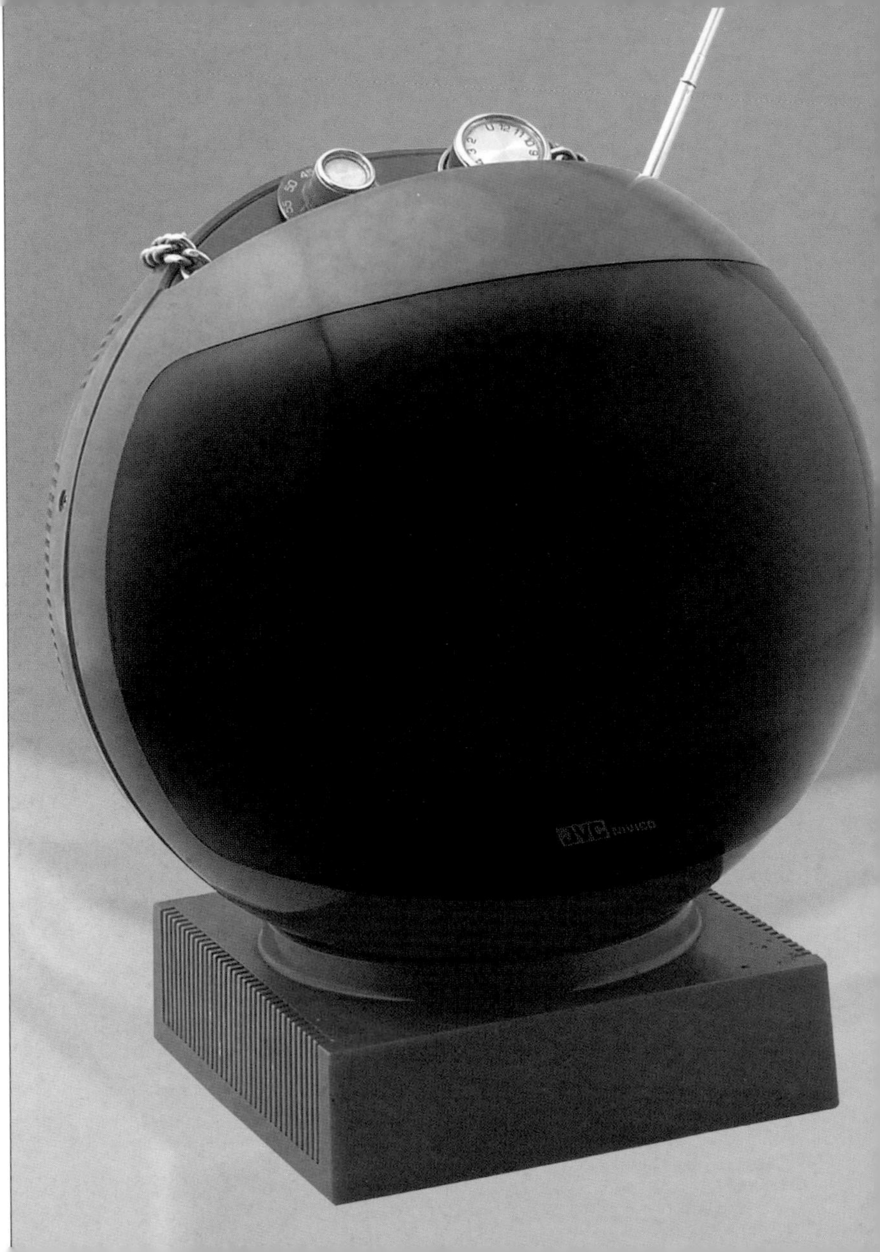

SPACE TV

When Neil Armstrong made "one small step for a man, one giant leap for mankind" and became the first person to set foot on the moon, the world went crazy for everything to do with outer space. Lunar capsules and space rockets were favorite toys, and sleek, futuristic design crept into even the most mundane of household objects, including dinner services, heaters, and televisions.

The design of this Videosphere television is clearly influenced by a spaceman's helmet and was known as "Sputnik," after the Russian satellite launch of 1957. This model was produced by JVC; it was made in red, black, and gray in the US, and white and orange in the UK. The controls are located at the top, along with a heavy chrome chain that allowed the set to be hung from the ceiling. Many versions have a radio and alarm clock in the base.

JVC Videosphere in molded plastic, made in the US. ★ ★ ★ ☆ ☆

Bush radio in cream and tan plastic. This radio was designed in 1959 and was made until the mid-1970s. ★★☆☆☆

RCA clock radio, with geometric ring design in blue and orange. ★☆☆☆☆

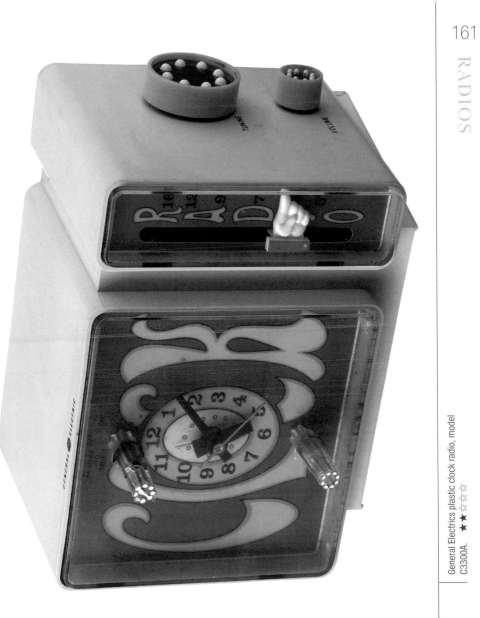

General Electrics plastic clock radio, model
C3300A. ★★☆☆☆

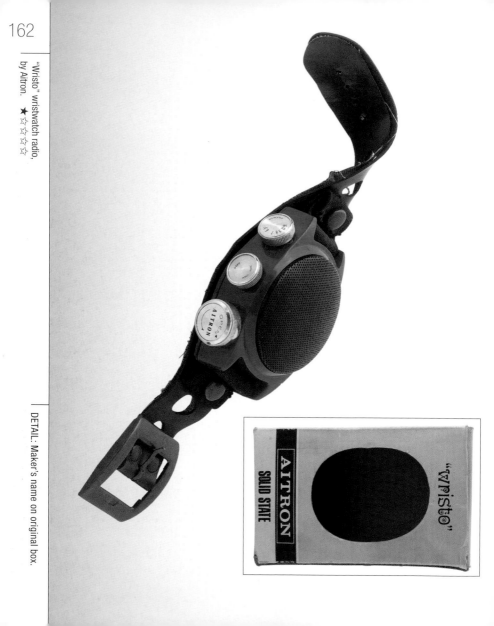

"Wristo" wristwatch radio, by Aitron. ★☆☆☆☆

DETAIL: Maker's name on original box.

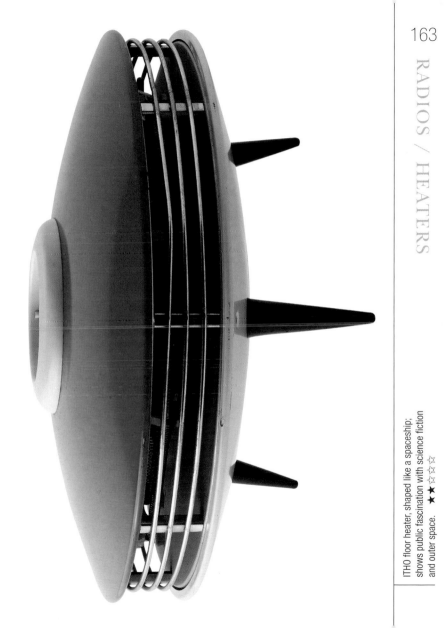

ITHO floor heater, shaped like a spaceship; shows public fascination with science fiction and outer space. ★ ☆ ☆ ☆

Dodo "Lord Kitchener" tin, with picture of Lord Kitchener on Union Flag background. ★☆☆☆☆

DETAIL: Maker's name on rim.

Tin tray with "Queen Anne Rare Scotch Whisky"
lithographed advertisement. ★ ☆ ☆ ☆

Associated Biscuits Ltd. tin with design based on "Swinging London" – an expression for the cultural trends centered in London in the 1960s. ★☆☆☆☆

Tin tray with "HAPPY" design by Peter Max. ★★☆☆☆

LORD KITCHENER

Lord Kitchener is best known for appearing as the heavily mustachioed face and pointing finger on the iconic "Your country needs you" First World War recruitment posters. During the 1960s, with everything British in fashion around the world, patriotic images from the past were once again in vogue. For this reason, a fashionable London shop, based on Portobello Road, was named "I was Lord Kitchener's Valet."

The shop specialized in vintage clothing and regimental uniforms, as well as modern products. Patronized by celebrities such as Jimi Hendrix, and representing an "alternative" street style, it used a logo depicting Lord Kitchener superimposed in a Pop Art style over the flag. Many of the shop's goods featured the Union Flag, with its association with "Swinging London," which was given a boost when England won the Soccer World Cup in 1966.

Small Lord Kitchener plate, marked "I was Lord Kitchener's Valet" on back. ★ ★ ☆ ☆ ☆

Set of drinks coasters by Ian Logan, made from laminated plastic over cork. ★ ☆☆☆☆

American tin tray with printed psychedelic design. ★ ☆☆☆☆

Marks & Spencer biscuit tin with "flower power" design. ★ ☆☆☆☆

German clock by Salvest, in plastic
with orange face. ★ ☆☆☆☆

Worcester Ware tin waste paper bin, with lithographed "flower power" design. ★ ☆☆☆☆

Tin document storage box, with printed "flower power" design. ★ ☆☆☆☆

Picnic set, including flasks and cups, with plastic carrier. ★ ☆☆☆☆

MELLOW YELLOW

p.105

p.243

p.139

p.51

p.281

p.105

p.47

p.209

p.291

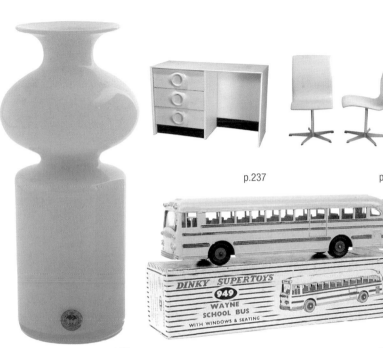

p.237

p.217

p.78

p.376

p.249

p.302

p.335

p.172

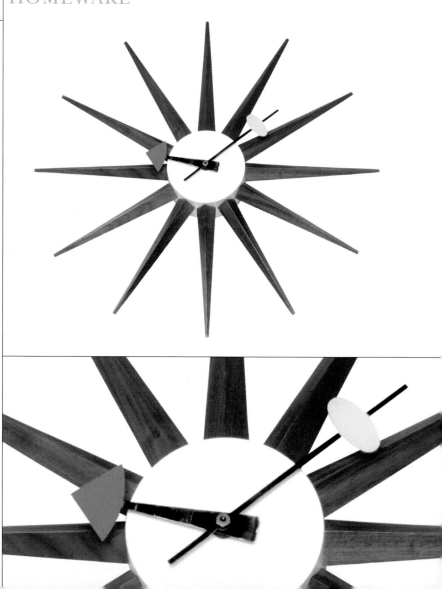

"Starburst" clock, designed by George Nelson, in aluminum and walnut, with Herman Miller label. ★★☆☆☆

Candlestick sculpture by Nagel, comprising sections that can be assembled into any combination. ★ ★ ☆ ☆ ☆

"A time for love,
a time for hate,
a time for peace,
I swear it's not too late."

THE BYRDS

Inflatable plastic coat hanger with printed design of bubbles and the word "LOVE." ★ ☆☆☆☆

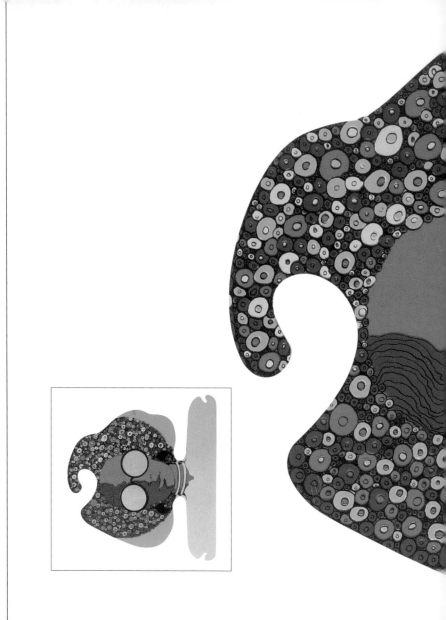

American coathanger in plastic, with design of woman wearing mirror lenses. ☆☆☆ ★★

Cover of American musical photo album in printed vinyl, by Annabel. ★★☆☆☆

"I love Los Angeles. I love Hollywood. They're beautiful. Everybody's plastic, but I love plastic. I want to be plastic."

ANDY WARHOL

First page of American musical photo album in printed vinyl, by Annabel; has original box. ★★☆☆☆

FURNITURE

By looking at everyday objects in radical and futuristic ways, designers in the US and Europe began to develop innovative designs for the home. The use of revolutionary materials and processes, as well as bold colors and fantastic new shapes, made 1960s furniture fun, stylish, and practical.

The new "throwaway" society embraced affordable furniture in man-made materials, such as plastic seating. The Pop culture characteristics of youthfulness and leisure were reflected in fun furniture such as the inflatable "Blow" chair. Lighting design was also influenced by contemporary fashions, and high street shops sold everything from inexpensive copies of the latest designer classics to self-assembly paper lampshades.

Artificial materials, such as glass fiber and PVC, favored by fashionable designers, were, however, prone to damage. Key designs were a popular way to add a period touch to the home.

Eero Aarnio "Ball/Globe" chair, for Akso, in fiberglass polyester, with white lacquered aluminum base and original cushions and upholstery. *1966* ★★★★★

Eero Aarnio green polyester chair "pastilli," for Asko Oy, Helsinki,
Finland. *c.1967* ★★ ☆☆☆

Henrik Thor-Larsen "Ovalia" chair, for Torlan, Staffanstorp, Sweden, in black fiberglass plastic, with an aluminum foot. ★★★★☆

Günter Beltzig "Floris" chairs, by Beltzig Design, with artist's signature in felt-tip pen, in molded fiberglass resin; handmade in two parts.   c. 1967   ★★★★

Eero Saarinen "Womb Chair" for Knoll International in lacquered tubular steel, with fiberglass seat and cellular cushions.   ★★★★

Bernard Rancillac, "Elephant Chair," for Galerie Lacloche, Paris, with artist's signature, in yellow fiberglass-reinforced polyester and black-enameled, flat-rolled steel. *1966* ★★★★★

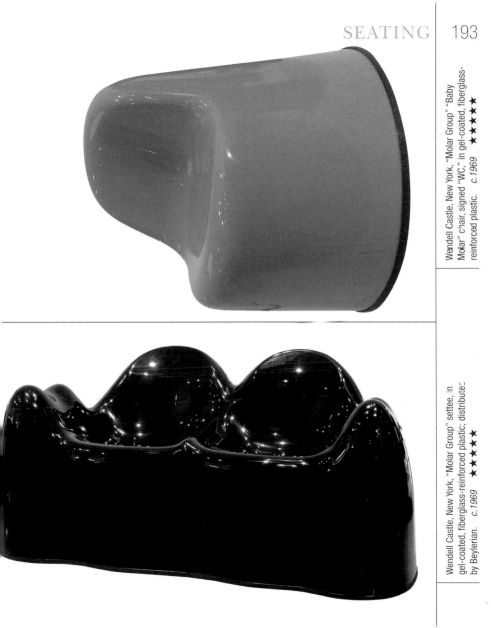

Wendell Castle, New York, "Molar Group" "Baby Molar" chair, signed "WC," in gel-coated, fiberglass-reinforced plastic. c.1969 ★★★★★

Wendell Castle, New York, "Molar Group" settee, in gel-coated, fiberglass-reinforced plastic; distributed by Beylerian. c.1969 ★★★★★

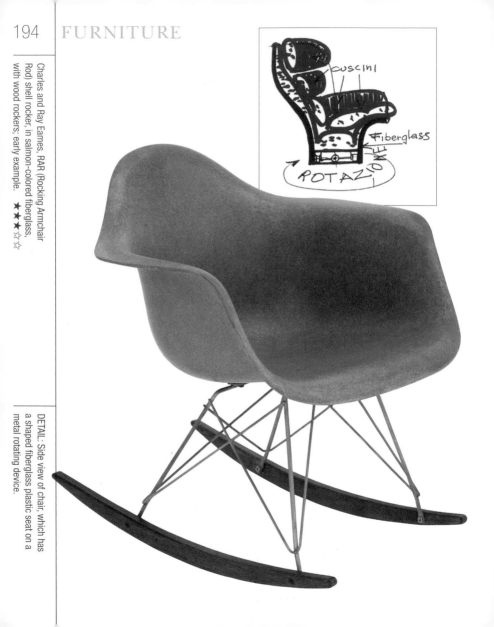

Charles and Ray Eames, RAR (Rocking Armchair Rod) shell rocker, in salmon-colored fiberglass, with wood rockers; early example. ★★★☆☆

DETAIL: Side view of chair, which has a shaped fiberglass plastic seat on a metal rotating device.

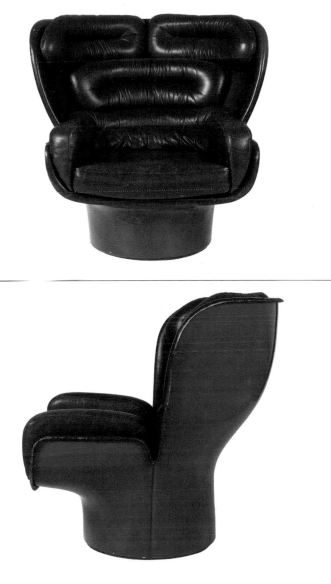

Joe Colombo "Elda Chair," for Comfort Milan. It has leather covered, cellular rubber cushions, fixed with metal hooks.   *c.1964*   ★★★★ ★★

Gionatan De Pas inflatable "Blow" chair, for Zanotta, Milan, in welded PVC.
1967 ★★☆☆☆

1964 World Fair concept chair, in red and white enameled wood; unmarked. ★★★★★

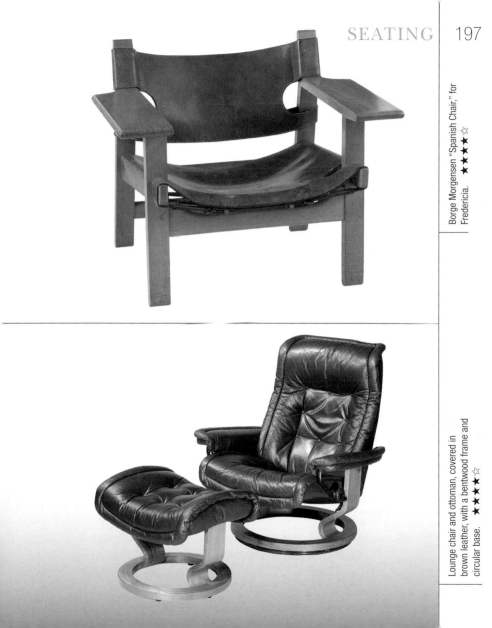

Borge Morgensen "Spanish Chair," for Fredericia. ★★★☆

Lounge chair and ottoman, covered in brown leather, with a bentwood frame and circular base. ★★★☆

FUNKY FORMS

p.200

p.248

p.214

p.215

p.94

p.210

p.210

p.79

p.67

p.86

p.94

p.108

Arne Jacobson tan leather "Egg Chair," for Fritz Hansen, which combines modernist ideals with Nordic naturalism. It was designed for the SAS hotel in Copenhagen. ★★★★★

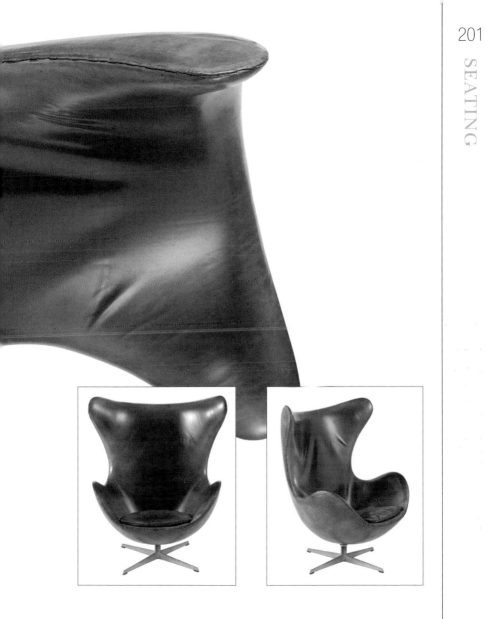

George Nakashima walnut lounge chairs, with loose cushions (not shown). *c.1966* ★★★★★★

Norman Cherner chair, for Plycraft, with bentwood arms and legs and orange upholstered seat and back; has partial paper label. ★★★☆

Mies van der Rohe "Barcelona" chairs, for Seagram Collection, one with the Seagram label, with leather upholstery on chrome metal frame. ★★★★★★

Jorgen Hovelskov "Harp" chair, for Christensen and
Larsen, with ebonized frame and synthetic string flag
back. ★ ★ ★ ★ ☆

Charles Eames wire side
chair. *c.1960*

★★★★☆

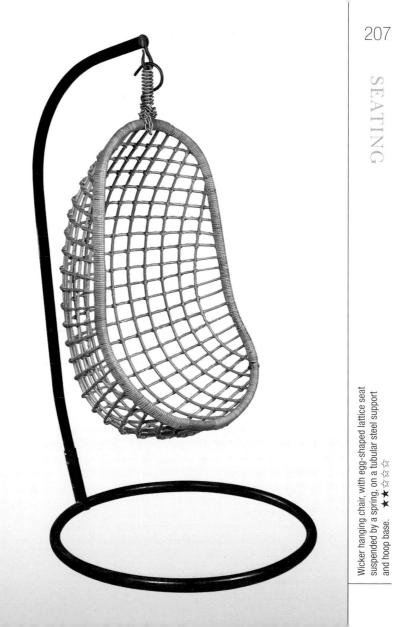

SEATING

Wicker hanging chair, with egg-shaped lattice seat suspended by a spring, on a tubular steel support and hoop base. ★★☆☆☆

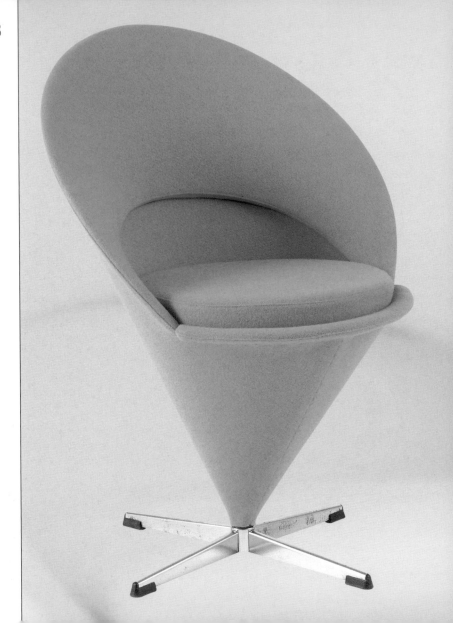

VERNER PANTON

The revolutionary approach of Danish designer Verner Panton (1926–98) resulted in innovative, exciting designs that reflected an optimistic belief in the future and mirrored the playfulness of the 1960s.

After studying at the Royal Danish Academy in Copenhagen, Panton established his own studio and became known for his radical architectural proposals as well as his furniture and textiles. He said of himself: "By experimenting with lighting, colors, textiles, and furniture and utilizing the latest technologies, I try to show new ways, to encourage people to use their fantasy and make their surroundings more exciting."

When Panton designed his futuristic "Cone" chair, he divorced himself from any preconceived notions of what a chair should look like. The chair, originally made for his parents' restaurant, Komigen (Come Again), on the island of Funen, proved so popular that it was put into production by Plus-Linje.

"Cone" chair by Verner Panton, with yellow cover. ★★★ ☆☆

Verner Panton stool from Plus Linje, Copenhagen's "K" series, with a sheet steel foot and loose cushion, upholstered in green; unmarked. ★★★☆☆

Verner Panton "Pyramid Cone" chair, for Plus Linje, Copenhagen, in sheet iron, with chrome plated steel pedestal and white plastic gliders. *c.1960* ★★★★★

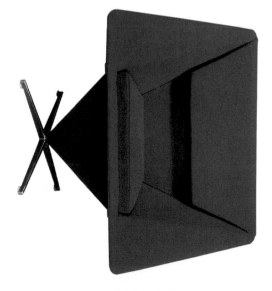

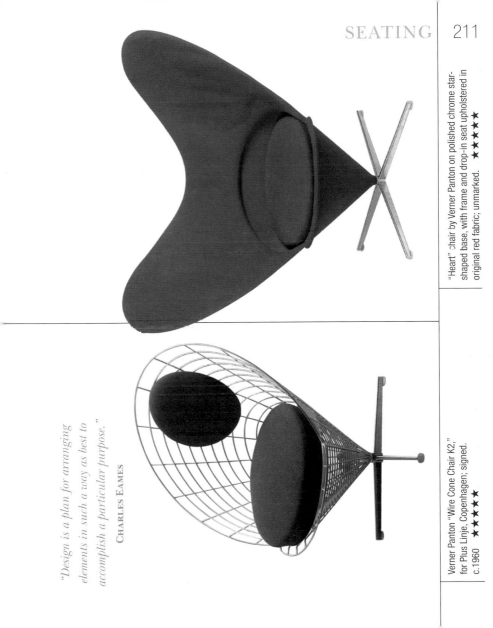

"Heart" chair by Verner Panton on polished chrome star-shaped base, with frame and drop-in seat upholstered in original red fabric; unmarked. ★★★★

"Design is a plan for arranging elements in such a way as best to accomplish a particular purpose."

CHARLES EAMES

Verner Panton "Wire Cone Chair K2," for Plus Linje, Copenhagen; signed. c.1960 ★★★★

These chairs echo the lines on Panton's 1960s molded plastic stacking chair.

Three "System 1-2-3," chairs by Verner Panton, for Fritz Hansen, Denmark. ★★★★

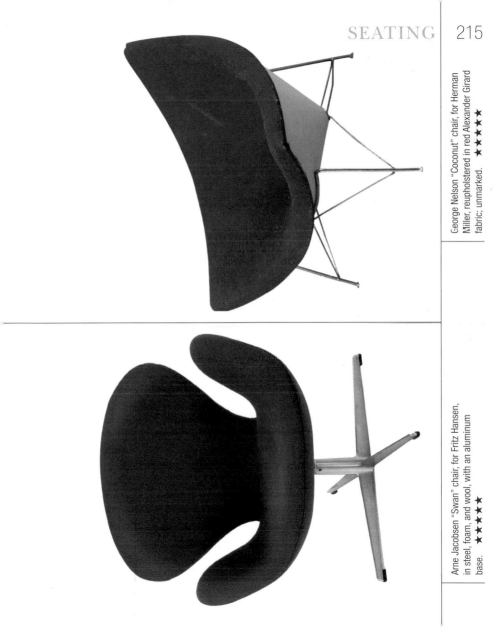

George Nelson "Coconut" chair, for Herman Miller, reupholstered in red Alexander Girard fabric; unmarked. ★★★★

Arne Jacobsen "Swan" chair, for Fritz Hansen, in steel, foam, and wool, with an aluminum base. ★★★★★

Geoffrey D. Harcourt "London Combination Corner Chair," for Artifort, Maastricht; signed "Artifort." Has purple woolen fabric upholstery and lacquered aluminum legs. ★★★★☆

Bruno Mathsson "Jetson II prototyp" chairs, for Karl Mathsson, with chrome-plated base. ★ ★ ★ ☆ ☆

Arne Jacobsen "Oxford" chairs on swiveling steel bases, for Fritz Hansen; have original leather upholstery, labels, and factory tags. ★ ★ ★ ★ ★

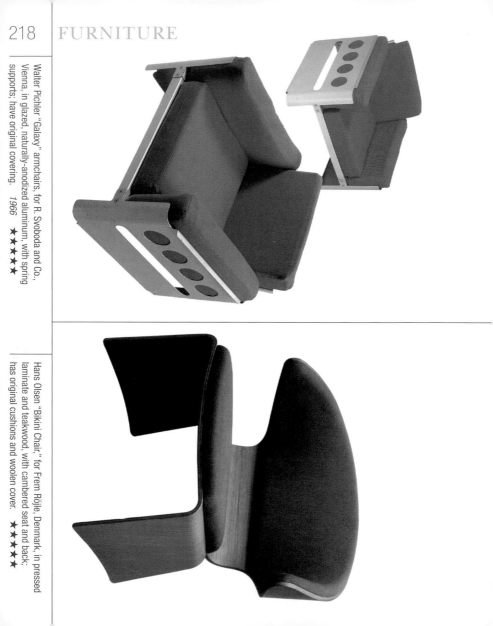

Walter Pichler "Galaxy" armchairs, for R. Svoboda and Co., Vienna, in glazed, naturally-anodized aluminum, with spring supports; have original covering. 1966 ★★★★★

Hans Olsen "Bikini Chair," for Frem Röjle, Denmark, in pressed laminate and teakwood, with cambered seat and back; has original cushions and woolen cover. ★★★★★

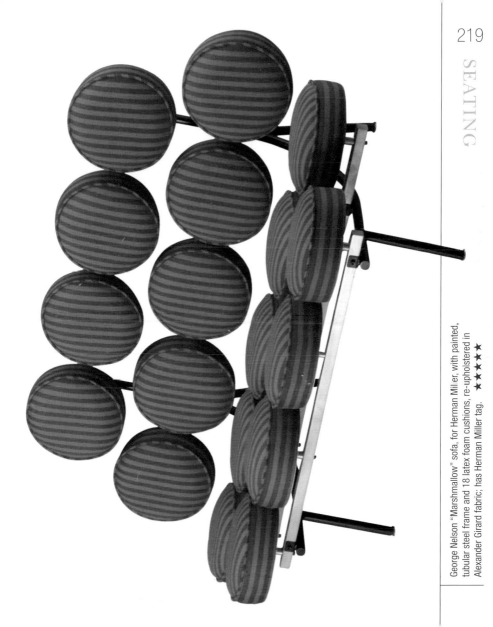

George Nelson "Marshmallow," sofa, for Herman Miller, with painted, tubular steel frame and 18 latex foam cushions, re-upholstered in Alexander Girard fabric; has Herman Miller tag.

★★★★

Foam settee, with stretch fabric cover in yellow, black, green, and white psychedelic pattern; unmarked. ★★★☆☆

Oskar Hodosi "fleur" seat object, in polyurethane and cellular material. Produced by Jodbauer, Vienna, for the furniture fair at Cologne, Germany. *1969* ★★★★★

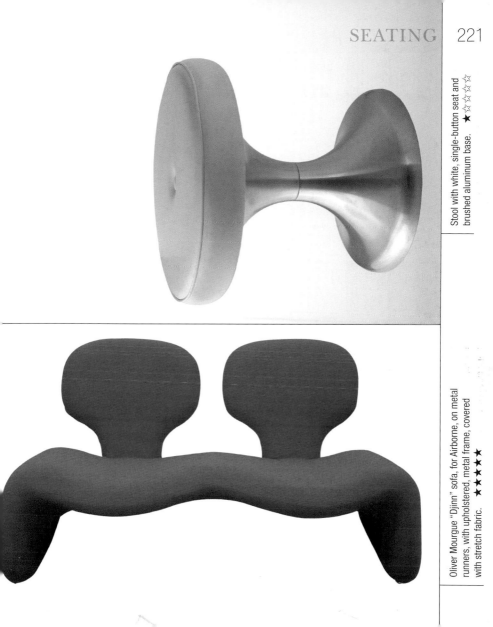

Stool with white, single-button seat and brushed aluminum base. ★ ☆ ☆ ☆

Oliver Mourgue "Djinn" sofa, for Airborne, on metal runners, with upholstered, metal frame, covered with stretch fabric. ★ ★ ★ ★

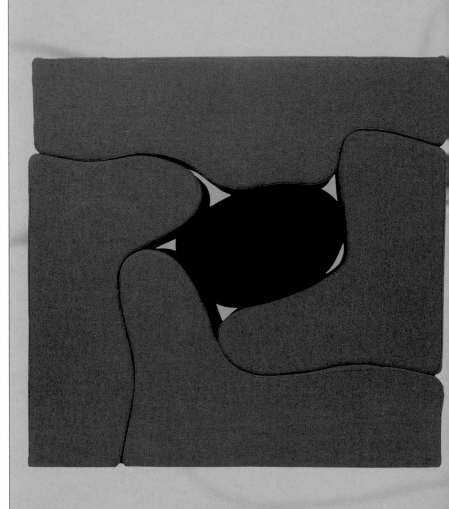

DETAIL: System fits together to become artwork.

MALITTE

The brainchild of the surrealist painter Roberto Sebastian Matta (1911–2002), the unconventional "Malitte" modular seating system encouraged flexible interior design. Developed in 1966 and named after Matta's wife, the system had four different seating elements and a circular middle section that could be used as a stool. The sculptural design particularly suited the minimalist interiors that became increasingly fashionable in the late 1960s. Its unusual form challenged the traditional concept of the three-piece suite and suggested an informal approach to sitting and interacting, indicative of the relaxed modern lifestyle.

Matta exploited the potential of polyurethane foam in creating the system, which was conceived to be suitable for high-volume manufacturing. The Malitte system was originally produced by Gavina; Knoll International took over production in 1968.

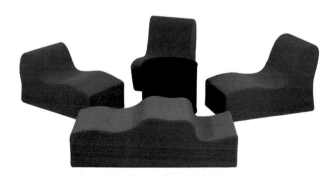

"Malitte" modular seating system, made by Gavina, Italy; has original woolen covers in light and dark blue. *1966* ★★★★★

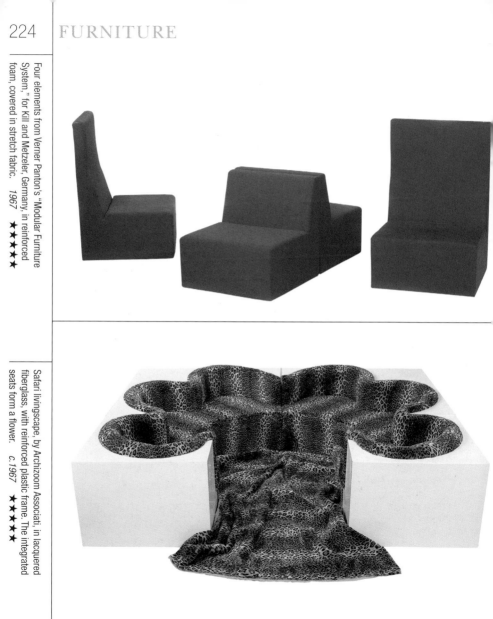

Four elements from Verner Panton's "Modular Furniture System," for Kill and Metzeler, Germany, in reinforced foam, covered in stretch fabric. *1967* ★★★★★

Safari livingscape, by Archizoom Associati, in lacquered fiberglass, with reinforced plastic frame. The integrated seats form a flower. *c.1967* ★★★★★

Joe Colombo "Tubo" modular seating system, for Flexform'
Prima. *1969* ★★★★

DETAIL: The table top has a detachable swiveling gray plastic tray.

The table top is made of
synthetic material, and the
metal base is on castors.

Austrian coffee table, on a metal base
in the shape of a cross. ☆ ★★★

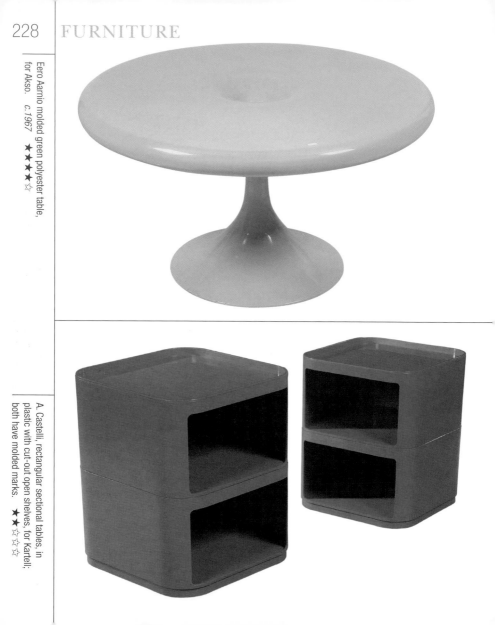

Eero Aarnio molded green polyester table, for Akso. *c.1967* ★★★★☆

A. Castelli, rectangular sectional tables, in plastic with cut-out open shelves, for Kartell; both have molded marks. ★★☆☆☆

Piero Fornasetti foldable "Map" table, with black enameled metal frame and table-top with polychrome varnish has manufacturer's label. ★★★☆

FURNITURE

Joe Colombo "Poker" card table, with white-layered plastic laminate top, removable, leather trimmed green baize, and stainless steel legs. *1968* ★★★★★

George Nakashima black walnut dining table, in hickory and rosewood; marked with client's name underneath. ★★★★★

FANTASTIC PLASTIC

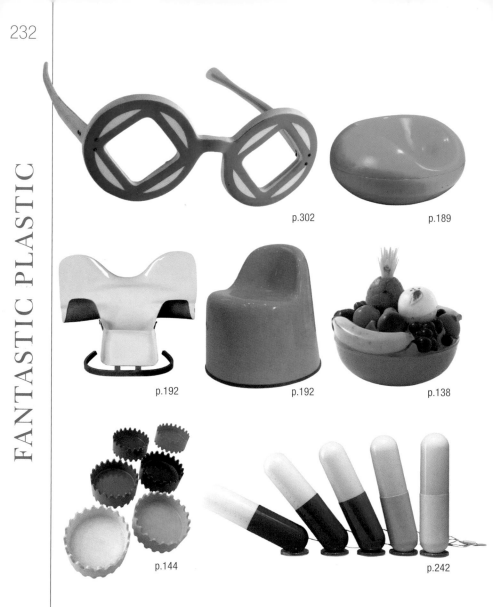

p.302

p.189

p.192

p.192

p.138

p.144

p.242

p.430

p.294

p.227

p.235

p.153

p.182

p.396

p.318

FANTASTIC PLASTIC

The table is made of fiberglass-reinforced plastic.

"Molar Group" swivel coffee table, designed and manufactured by Wendell Castle, Rochester, New York, in black gel-coated fiberglass-reinforced plastic. *c.1969* ★★★★

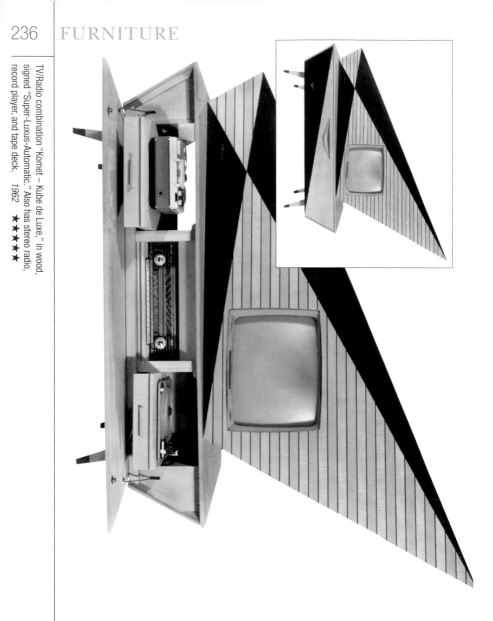

TV/Radio combination "Komet – Kube de Luxe," in wood, signed "Super-Luxus-Automatic." Also has stereo radio, record player, and tape deck. *1962* ★★★★★

Pop Art desk, with white laminate top and sides, and three molded yellow plastic drawers. ★★★☆☆

Sideboard by Pierre Cardin, in wood with black laminate and aluminum. ★★★★

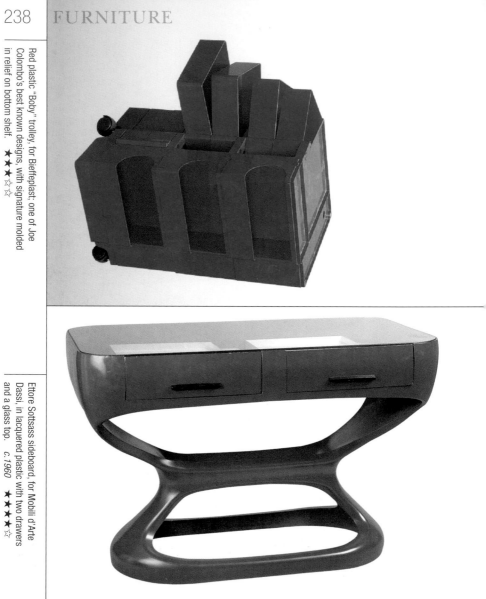

Red plastic "Boby" trolley, for Bieffeplast; one of Joe Colombo's best known designs, with signature molded in relief on bottom shelf. ★★★☆☆

Ettore Sottsass sideboard, for Mobili d'Arte Dassi, in lacquered plastic with two drawers and a glass top. *c.1960* ★★★★☆

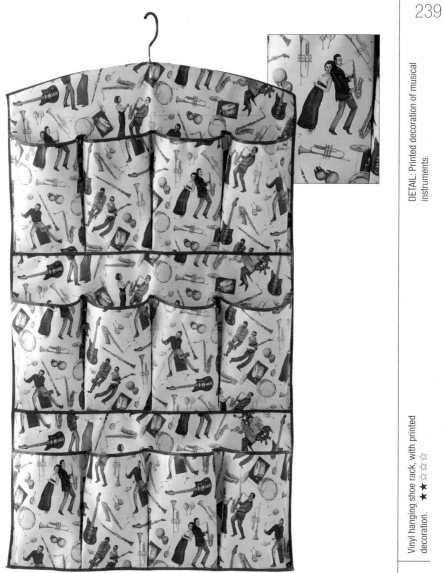

DETAIL: Printed decoration of musical instruments.

Vinyl hanging shoe rack, with printed decoration. ★ ☆ ☆ ☆

The commode is made of plastic-coated plywood.

Commode from the series "DF2000," by Raymond Loewy, for Doubinski Frères, Paris. 1965

★★★ ☆☆

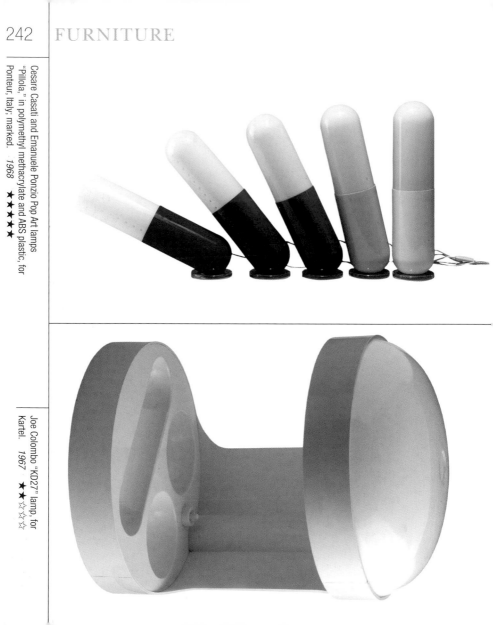

Cesare Casati and Emanuele Ponzio Pop Art lamps "Pillola," in polymethyl methacrylate and ABS plastic, for Ponteur, Italy; marked. *1968* ★★★★★

Joe Colombo "KD27" lamp, for Kartel. *1967* ★★☆☆☆

Cosmo Designs chrome table lamp, with four-piece, revolving shade. ★☆☆☆

Tobia Scarpa hanging lamp, with fiberglass skin mounted on a wire frame. *c.1968* ★★★☆

SHATTALINE LAMP

The huge variety of lighting produced during the 1960s reflected designers' desire to escape traditional forms of lighting such as the overhead ceiling lamp. By employing modern materials such as plastic, paper, and metal, as well as new shapes, they showed that lighting was no longer just for simple illumination, but could be used to create an appealing atmosphere in the home. Shapes were highly influenced by Pop Art, the Space Age, and other fashions.

The mass-produced Shattaline lamps were made from 1968 onwards for the affordable British retail chain British Home Stores (est. 1928). The base is made of cast resin and was produced in amber, green, and blue, in three different sizes. The shades had to be purchased separately, and were available in gold, orange, red, stone, or turquoise, to match a variety of interior color schemes.

Shattaline lamp with turquoise plastic resin base and yellow shade made of spun fiberglass. *c.1968* ★ ☆ ☆ ☆ ☆

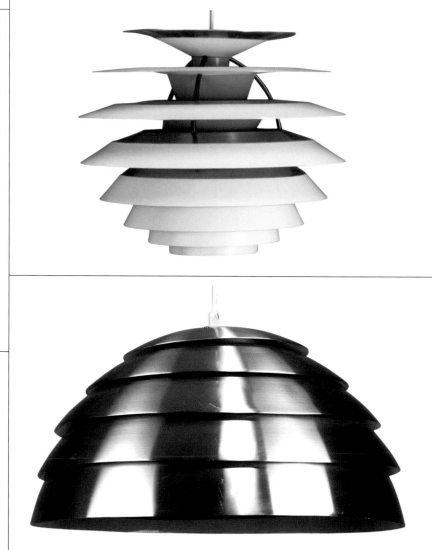

Poul Henningsen "PH contrax" hanging lamp, for Louis Poulsen, with aluminum and white enamel; has ceiling clamp; unmarked. ★★★★☆

Arne Jacobsen lamp, possibly made by Ateljé Lyktan, Sweden, with aluminum fins, lacquered white inside. ★★☆☆☆

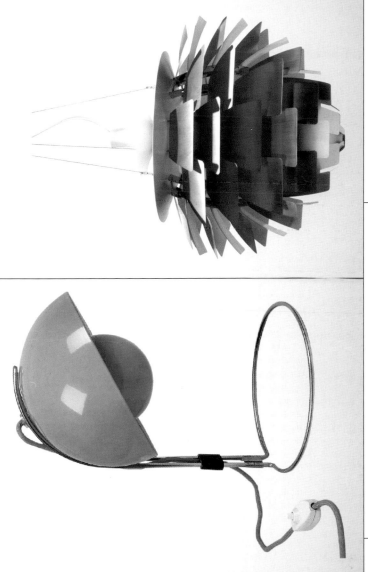

Poul Henningsen "Artichoke" lamp, for Louis Poulsen, in copper and steel. ★★★★★

"Flowerpot" table lamp, no. 23410, by Verner Panton for Louis Poulsen, in tubular steel, with orange lacquered mobile metal reflector. *1968* ★★★☆☆

FURNITURE

"Fun 1 DM" ceiling lamp by Verner Panton, for J. Luber AG; unmarked. ★★★★★

Verner Panton "Pantella" desklight, for Louis Poulsen. ★★★☆☆

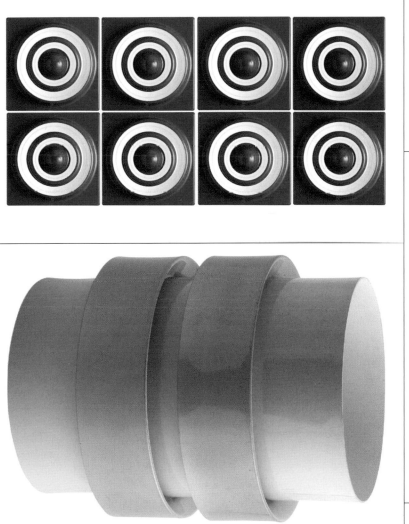

Eight Verner Panton "Ring Lamps," for Louis Poulsen, Denmark, in orange plastic. ★★★★

Five-tier ceiling light, of yellow and gray metal bands. ★☆☆☆

FASHION

New and outlandish modes of dress resulted from the exciting youth culture and radical ideas synonymous with the 1960s. Increased wealth enabled people to indulge their passion for fashion, and the trend for self-expression led to large-scale shopping for style-statement outfits and vintage clothes. Trends changed rapidly, meaning clothing had to be cheap and up to the minute rather than hardwearing and practical. Synthetic materials — and even paper — were extremely hip. Girls left their homes in mini skirts to parental cries of "you're not going out like that," while boys copied the collarless jackets and "mop-top" haircuts of The Beatles. Colors were bold and patterns were frantic, and the space race influenced the use of metallics and see-through plastics. Mary Quant, Pierre Cardin, and Emilio Pucci were some of the fashion names to aspire to. Later, the hippy look gained momentum and flower power took off.

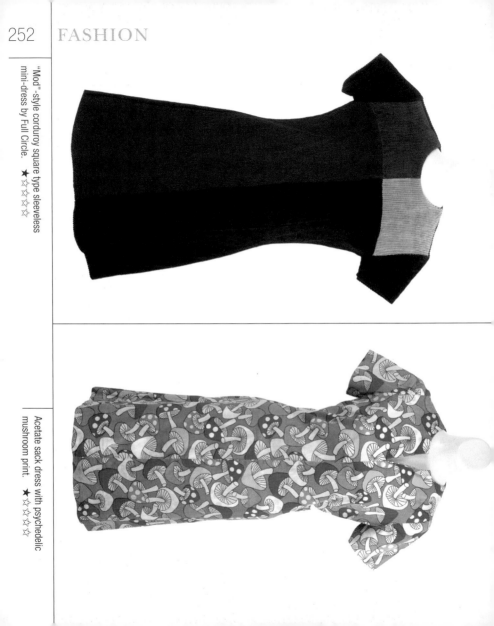

"Mod"-style corduroy square type sleeveless mini-dress by Full Circle. ★★☆☆☆

Acetate sack dress with psychedelic mushroom print. ★★☆☆☆

Pucci printed silk dress. ★★★☆☆

DETAIL: Pucci's signature "Emilio."

Yellow and green Lily Pulitzer sleeveless dress, with applied woven lace around neck and on pocket. ★★☆☆☆

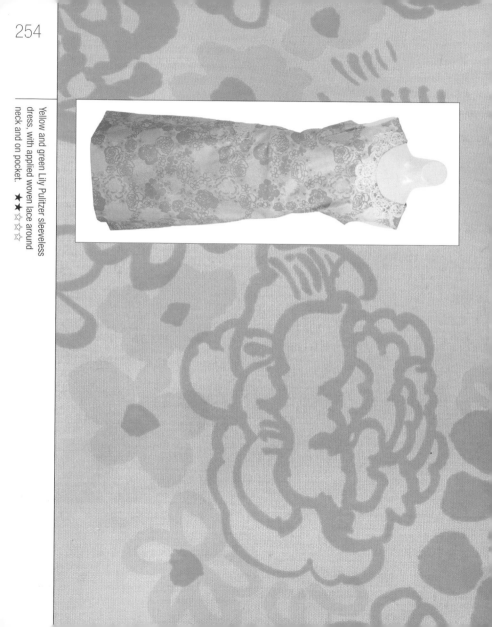

Printed polyester dress, decorated with Art Nouveau ladies' heads. The 1960s updated the Art Nouveau style in bright, psychedelic colors. ★ ☆ ☆ ☆

WARHOL

Known as the "Prince of Pop," Andy Warhol was one of the most important names in the Pop Art Movement. The 1960s was an extremely prolific decade for Warhol. His fascination with everyday, mass-produced, consumer objects, such as Campbell's Soup cans and Coca Cola bottles, manifested itself in his distinctive paintings. He once expressed his philosophy in one poignant sentence: "When you think about it, department stores are kind of like museums." Many works by Warhol remain icons of 20th century art, including silkscreen prints of famous celebrities such as Marilyn Monroe and Elizabeth Taylor.

Quick to cash in on its new cool status, Campbell's released the "Souper Dress," decorated with the company's distinctive soup cans, as an effective marketing device. Paper dresses such as this were all the rage, reflecting the "throwaway" aspects of popular culture and acknowledging the short-lived nature of modern fads.

Andy Warhol's "The Souper Dress," with label reading "The Souper Dress/ No Cleaning/ No Washing/ It's carefree fire resistant unless washed or cleaned/ To refreshen, press lightly with warm iron."   c.1960   ★★★☆ ★★★★

Ossie Clark velvet floral maxi skirt.
Late 1960s ★★★☆☆

Prestige of Boston "flower power" printed velvet skirt. ★☆☆☆☆

★☆☆☆

Italian "Mod" woven knit maxi skirt.

Pair of psychedelic flower printed pants. ★ ☆ ☆ ☆

LOOK FOR THE 〝〟 ON THE POCKET

TRADE MARK

Guaranteed

If this garment should prove defective in any way return it directly to us for replacement or refund at our option.

WRANGLER
GREENSBORO, NORTH CAROLINA

MADE IN U.S.A.

Wrangler

Trim
Western Fit

Pre-Shrunk

SLIM

SEE BACK FOR SIZE SCALES AND LAUNDRY INSTRUCTIONS

DETAIL: The original
card label.

Pair of Wrangler yellow and black printed
floral and polka dot jeans. ★ ☆☆☆

Aquamarine plush Christian Dior hat with netting
over colored feathers. ★☆☆☆

PUCCI

Nothing shouts 1960s textile design as loudly as the colorful clothing and accessories of Italian designer Emilio Pucci (1914–92). In 1949, Pucci opened his first boutique on the island of Capri, and his "Capri" pants took the world by storm. Becoming the kingpin of textile reinvention and beautiful prints in the 1960s, his designs revolutionized the world of fashion. His instantly recognizable clothes, with their bright tones and bold geometric patterns, are immensely wearable today and go through cycles of popularity every few years. As with many successful couturiers, several other manufacturers have copied Pucci's distinctive style, from the 1960s right through to the present day.

Pucci's designs included accessories and perfumes, but he is best-known for his use of brilliant colors in silks, underwear, scarves, and towels. Pieces are often signed. The current line of Pucci clothing is still in demand for today's fashion addicts. He is truly "The King of Casual Couture."

Pucci silk scarf in shades of blue, gray, and black, with geometric pattern. ★ ★ ☆ ☆ ☆

Pair of "flower power" printed silk shoes by "Schiaparelli Paris & New York." ★ ☆☆☆☆

Pair of Taj of India shocking pink silk shoes with clear soles. This style of shoe was Gloria Swanson's favorite. ★ ☆☆☆

"Paperdelic" four piece paper cloth beach outfit. ★ ☆ ☆ ☆ ☆

Estrava fabric bikini with Emilio Pucci design, decorated with fishes. ★ ★ ☆ ☆ ☆

Courrèges wet-look turquoise jacket. Although this futuristic material may look robust, it is quite fragile. ★ ★ ☆ ☆

An unopened tin of Carnaby Street-style "British Knickers." ★ ☆ ☆ ☆

☆☆☆☆ ★ Batik-style printed cotton jacket made in Hong Kong, with small lapels.

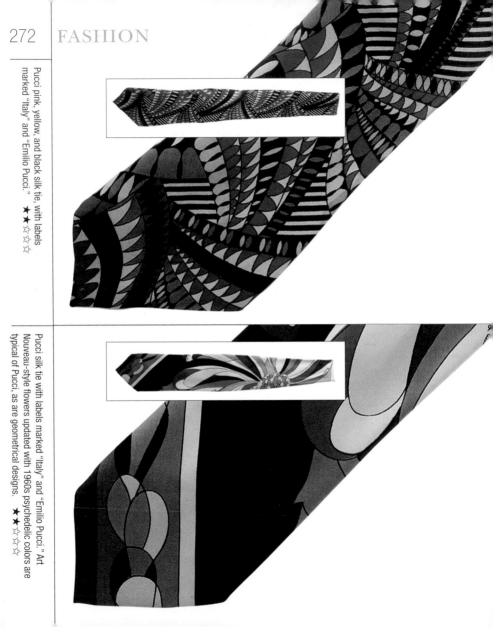

Pucci pink, yellow, and black silk tie, with labels marked "Italy" and "Emilio Pucci." ★★☆☆☆

Pucci silk tie with labels marked "Italy" and "Emilio Pucci." Art Nouveau-style flowers updated with 1960s psychedelic colors are typical of Pucci, as are geometrical designs. ★★☆☆☆

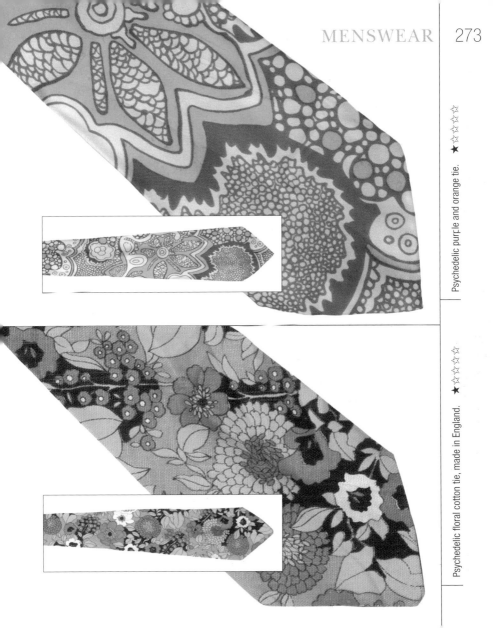

Psychedelic purple and orange tie. ★☆☆☆

Psychedelic floral cotton tie, made in England. ★☆☆☆

PSYCHEDELIA

p.346

p.340

p.349

p.357

p.357

p.157

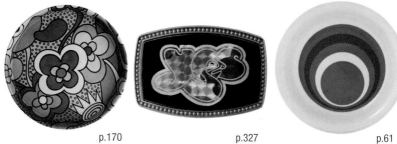

p.170

p.327

p.61

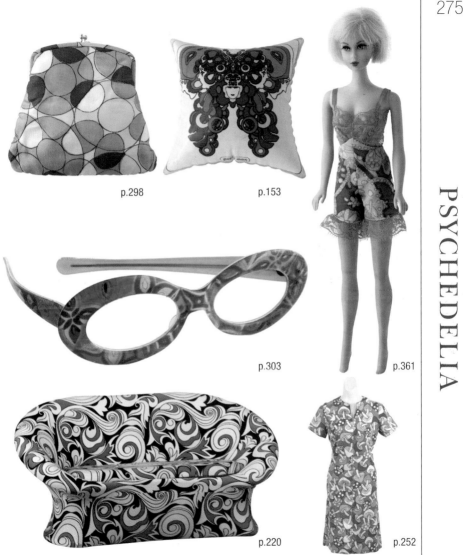

p.298

p.153

p.303

p.361

p.220

p.252

PSYCHEDELIA

Pair of Pop Art plastic "flower power" earrings, with semi-translucent petals and opaque deep purple centers; unsigned. ★☆☆☆☆

Pair of Pop Art black and green clip earrings with injection molded green dot. ★★☆☆☆

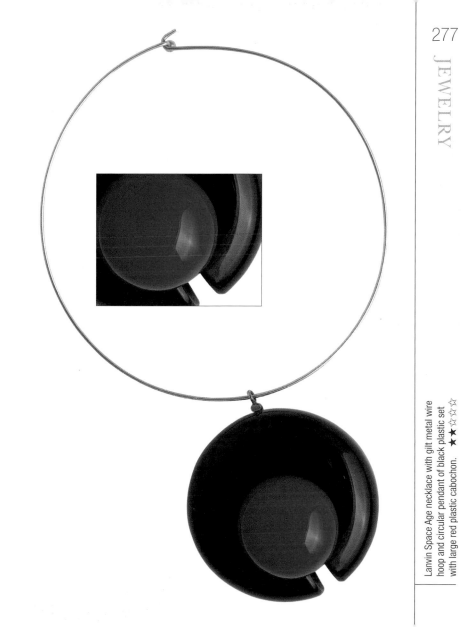

Lanvin Space Age necklace with gilt metal wire hoop and circular pendant of black plastic set with large red plastic cabochon. ★★☆☆

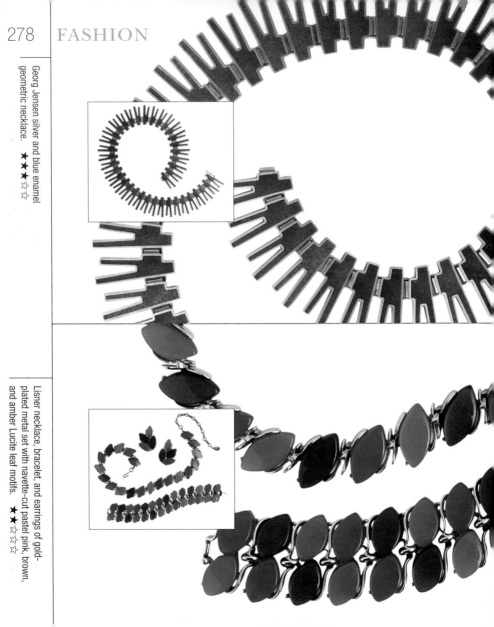

Georg Jensen silver and blue enamel geometric necklace. ★★★☆☆

Lisner necklace, bracelet, and earrings of gold-plated metal set with navette-cut pastel pink, brown, and amber Lucite leaf motifs. ★★☆☆☆

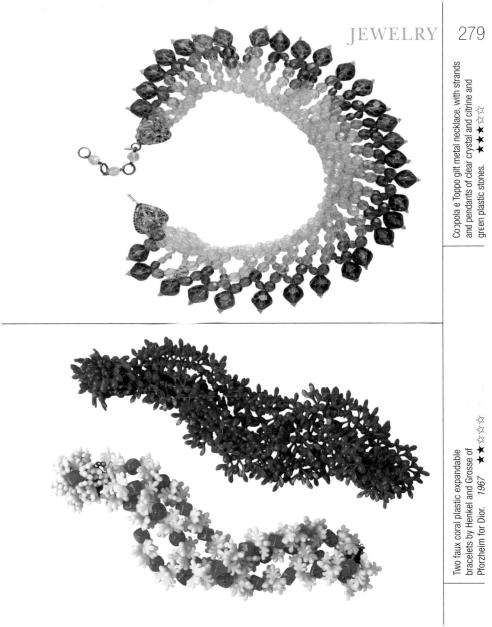

Coopola e Toppo gilt metal necklace, with strands and pendants of clear crystal and citrine and green plastic stones. ★★★☆

Two faux coral plastic expandable bracelets by Henkel and Grosse of Pforzheim for Dior. *1967* ★★☆☆

Stanley Hagler bib-of-bees necklace with
hand-wired topaz crystal octagons and
amber glass beads. ★★★☆☆

Pop Art yellow Bakelite necklace. ★ ★ ☆ ☆

Whiting & Davis silver-plated coiled snake bangle, with expandable mesh wrist band and solid punched and engraved head. ★ ☆ ☆ ☆

FASHION

Stanley Hagler floral pin, with petals and leaves of gilt metal, clear crystal rhinestones, blue and turquoise pressed glass, and faux seed pearls. ★ ★ ☆ ☆ ☆

Stanley Hagler fruit and leaf pin in cherry red, yellow, black, and green Murano glass. ★ ☆ ☆ ☆ ☆

Stanley Hagler Christmas tree pin, with gilt basket, ruby baguette rhinestones, and emerald glass beads. ★★☆☆

Stanley Hagler flower pin, with red and green Murano glass leaves and petals, and a yellow glass cabochon center. ★★☆☆

Warner flower pin, with "day and night" (open-and-shut) mechanism of gold-tone metal. *c.1960* ★★★☆☆

Sarah Coventry bunny pin, in gold-tone metal with one ruby glass cabochon eye and a garnet glass cabochon nose. ★☆☆☆☆

Unsigned hummingbird gold-plated metal pin with turquoise Lucite rings and aquamarine crystal rhinestone eyes. ★ ☆ ☆ ☆ ☆

Six clear and colored laminated Lucite fashion rings. These rings would have been retailed in boutiques such as Biba in London. ★ ★ ☆ ☆ ☆

FASHION

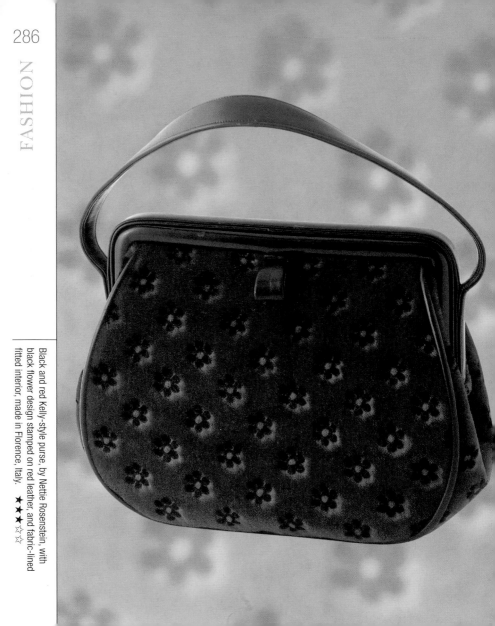

Black and red Kelly-style purse, by Nettie Rosenstein, with black flower design stamped on red leather, and fabric-lined fitted interior, made in Florence, Italy. ★★★☆☆

NETTIE ROSENSTEIN

Austrian-born Nettie Rosenstein emigrated to the US as a child and began her career as a milliner in 1927. By the 1930s she was working as a fashion designer, and began to make glamorous purses and colorful costume jewelry to complement her clothes. Her couture designs were featured in a number of high-profile newspapers and magazines throughout the Sixties.

In 1961, she moved away from clothing to concentrate on her accessory lines. Nettie Rosenstein's purses were made in the Italian city of Florence, a place renowned for its high-quality leather goods.

Black lizard and leather purse by Hermès. This famous design was called "The Piano Bag." ★★★★★★

DETAIL: The golden stamp "Hermès Paris MADE IN FRANCE."

Black calfskin leather purse, by De Leon, USA; elongated circular design with satin lining. A classic 1960s design. ★★☆☆☆

Yellow faux crocodile leather purse, with gold tone clasp. ★ ☆☆☆

Turquoise alligator box purse by Nettie Rosenstein, with restored clasp and mirror, made in Florence, Italy. ★★★★☆

American Holzman purse, with geometric design created using silkscreen on leather, wrapped frame with piped edges, silk lining, and ball clasp; signed "Holzman." ★★☆☆☆

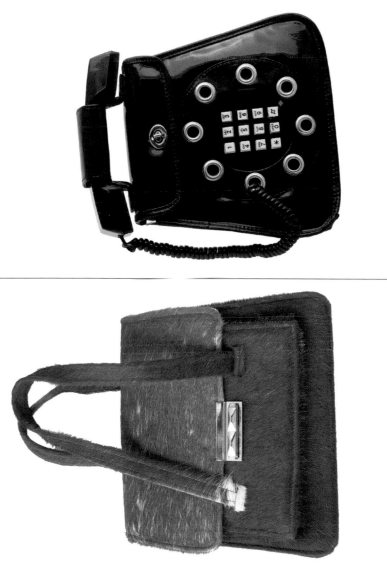

American "Telephone" purse in patent leather with embossed design: by plugging it into a socket, calls could actually be made from it. ★ ★ ★ ☆ ☆

Brown pony-skin purse with two handles and gilt metal clasp. ★ ★ ★ ☆ ☆

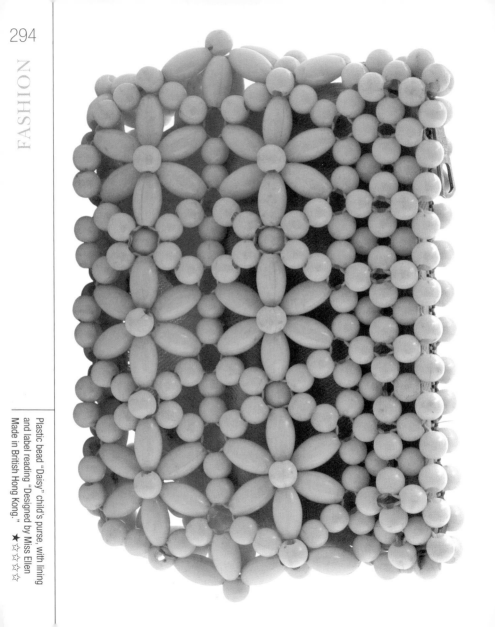

Plastic bead "Daisy" child's purse, with lining and label reading "Designed by Miss Ellen Made in British Hong Kong." ★ ☆☆☆☆

Enid Collins printed and plastic jeweled "By The Roadside" purse, interior marked with Collins logo and "Copyright The Original Collins of Texas." ★ ☆☆☆☆

Colorful velvet purse with waterfall front by
Pucci. ★★★★☆

Colorful purse, unsigned, with matching clutch.

☆☆☆ ★★

Colorful purse by Ingber, USA, decorated
with psychedelic circles. This bag is classic
1960s in style and design. ★★☆☆☆

Multicolored purse and matching shoes, by Hemphill Wells Geppetto, in Geppetto box. ★ ☆☆☆☆

DETAIL: The graphics on the box are brightly colored, amusing, and typical of the 1960s.

GEPPETTO
...of course

PRETTY WOMAN

p.285

p.292

p.283

p.292

p.305

p.288

p.254

p.305

p.258

p.299

p.279

p.266

p.263

p.255

p.267

p.284

p.309

p.279

Pair of French gold and black laminated plastic "bug" sunglasses. ★ ★ ☆ ☆ ☆

Pair of Op Art green fabric and laminated plastic sunglasses, the arm stamped "FRANCE." ★ ★ ☆ ☆ ☆

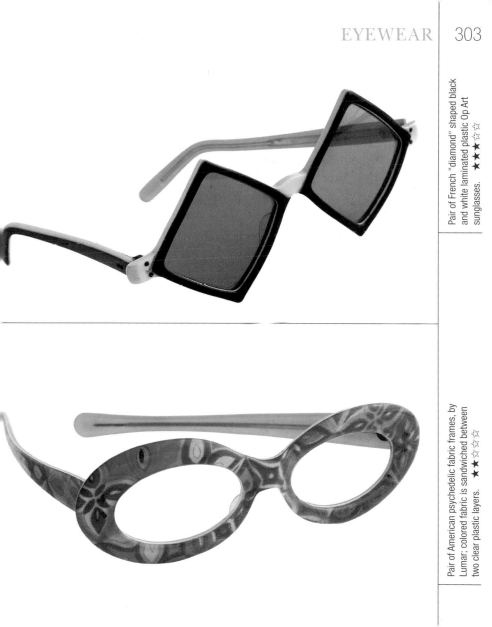

Pair of French "diamond" shaped black and white laminated plastic Op Art sunglasses. ★ ★ ★ ☆ ☆

Pair of American psychedelic fabric frames, by Lumar; colored fabric is sandwiched between two clear plastic layers. ★ ★ ☆ ☆ ☆

Pair of Pierre Cardin smoky gray plastic "lips" frames, the arms stamped "Pierre Cardin MADE IN FRANCE." ★★★☆☆

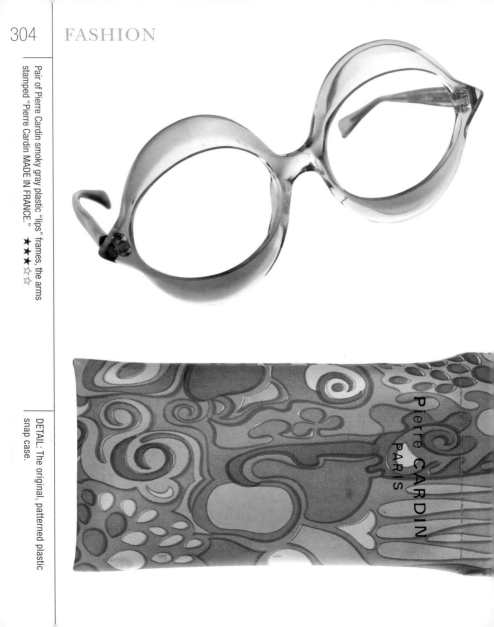

DETAIL: The original, patterned plastic snap case.

Pair of Pierre Cardin transparent brown plastic "eyebrow" sunglasses, the arms stamped "Pierre CARDIN." ★ ★ ☆ ☆

Pair of French laminated, pearlized, rust-colored, plastic bow tie-shaped spectacles, the arm stamp and paper label reading "REGGAE." ★ ★ ☆ ☆

Pair of French Op Art black and white checkerboard molded plastic sunglasses, the arm stamped "FRANCE." ★ ★ ☆ ☆ ☆

Italian "CIR" printed fabric sticker,
depicting a man in a hat, printed "CIR
TORINO MADE IN ITALY." ★ ☆☆☆☆

BIBA

Behind the glamor of Barbara Hulanicki's Biba – the first mail order business for avant-garde fashion – was a nod to the Art Nouveau design movement. The black and gold logo, designed by John McConnell in 1966, typified the allure of Hulanicki's designs and featured the curvaceous forms, synomonous with the 1960s, but inspired by the earlier design movement.

Although in clear contrast to the futuristic fashion of many designers, the gentle colors and echoes of romanticism, attracted 100,000 visitors a week to Biba's London store on High Street, Kensington. Labeled "the most in shop" for girls by Time magazine in 1966, Hulanicki made use of vintage fabrics for style and economy – and prices were attractively low. Biba sold dresses in midi and maxi lengths, contrasting with Mary Quant's Bazaar boutique mini skirts. The cosmetics range, retailed through Dorothy Perkins, was also very successful. Popularity lasted into the mid-1970s, when the brand went into steady decline.

★ ★ ☆ ☆ ☆

Set of three Biba cosmetics containers.

★☆☆☆☆

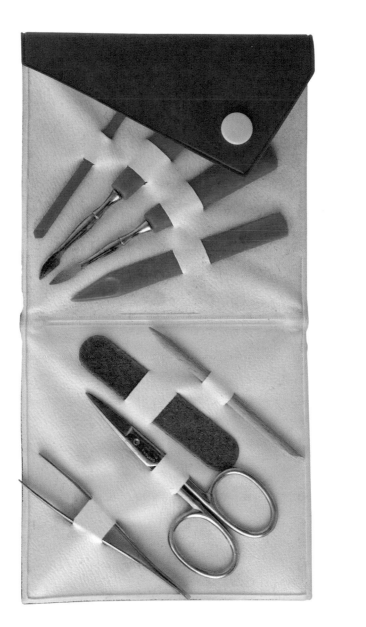

DETAIL: The inside of the manicure set.

REMEMBER THIS?

Moon landings, civil rights clashes, and student peace movements – the Sixties saw some of the most turbulent and iconic events of the 20th century. The young were set on changing society, and music became both their rallying call and an act of rebellion. Generations clashed over everything from politics to fashion and music, as teenagers turned up The Beatles or "tuned in and dropped out" at festivals such as Woodstock. Design reflected concerns of the period. Peace signs and flowers became popular symbols of love and unity while futuristic shapes reflected the fascination with the space race. Posters and ceramics commemorating popular events such as the "Summer of Love" and the moon landing, or objects with distinctive 1960s styling, are very popular today. Toys, particularly favorites such as Barbie or Action Man, appeal to nostalgic baby boomers and prices can be surprisingly high.

The Beatles, a membership booklet, with signatures, and a Cavern Club membership card.

Beatles memorabilia, including the album "All My Loving,"
a Parlaphone album, and a double single set and storybook
from the "Magical Mystery Tour." ★★★★☆

A Beatles rug in yellow, oranges, and black, shows the four faces of the group. ★★☆☆☆

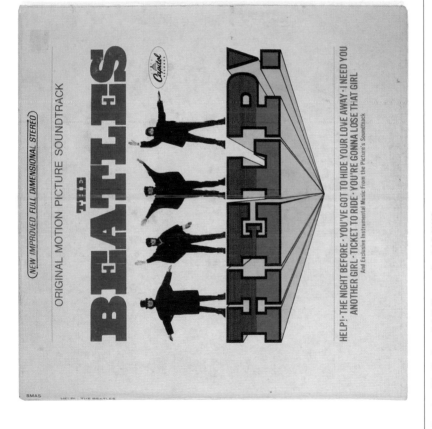

An American "The Beatles - Help!" film soundtrack LP, SMAS
2386, released by Capitol Records. *1965* ★★☆☆☆

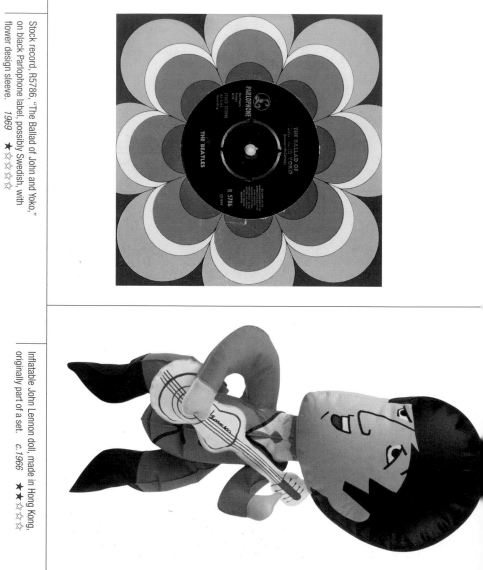

Stock record, R5786, "The Ballad of John and Yoko," on black Parlophone label, possibly Swedish, with flower design sleeve. *1969* ★☆☆☆☆

Inflatable John Lennon doll, made in Hong Kong, originally part of a set. *c.1966* ★★☆☆☆

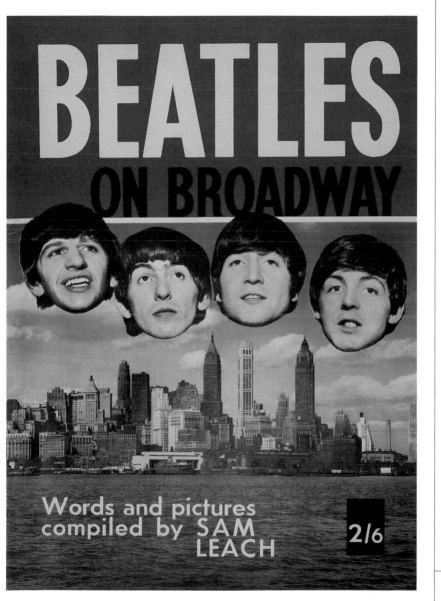

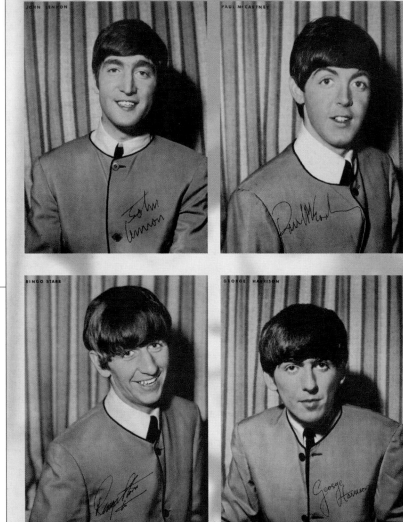

Set of four Beatles color printed publicity photographs, with facsimile signatures of John Lennon, Paul McCartney, Ringo Starr, and George Harrison. ★ ☆☆☆☆

THE BEATLES

The Beatles are still top of the rock-and-pop memorabilia league. Their first album "Meet the Beatles," released in 1964, became the fastest-selling LP in US recording history, and the "Fab Four," already pop heroes in the UK, took the US by storm. When they flew into New York's Kennedy Airport to appear on Ed Sullivan's television show and perform at Carnegie Hall they were greeted at the gate by thousands of screaming fans. The word Beatlemania had entered the language.

Fans on both sides of the Atlantic were overwhelmed with merchandise, and teenagers did not have to dig too deep to acquire such items. Almost everyone could afford an inflatable doll modeled on one of their idols, while those on larger budgets could choose from several ranges of clothing, school equipment, and games.

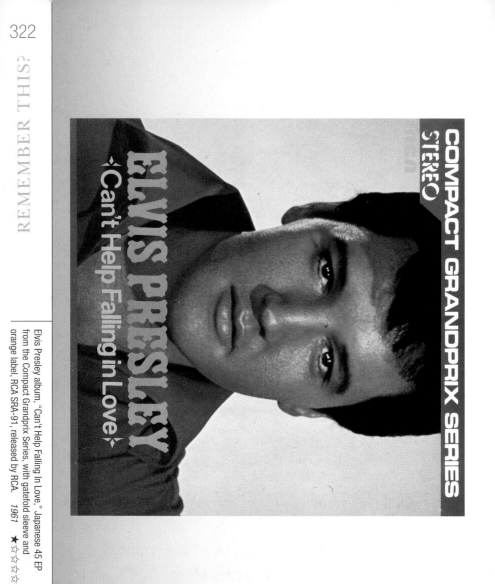

Elvis Presley album, "Can't Help Falling In Love," Japanese 45 EP from the Compact Grandprix Series, with gatefold sleeve and orange label, RCA SRA-91, released by RCA. *1961* ★☆☆☆☆

November edition of Photoplay magazine, featuring Elvis on the cover. *1962* ★ ☆ ☆ ☆

One-sided Christmas card reading "Seasons Greetings Elvis and the Colonel 1966," signed "To Mary from Elvis Presley." ★ ★ ☆ ☆

Rolling Stones souvenir booklet, containing pictures and features.
c.1965 ★☆☆☆☆

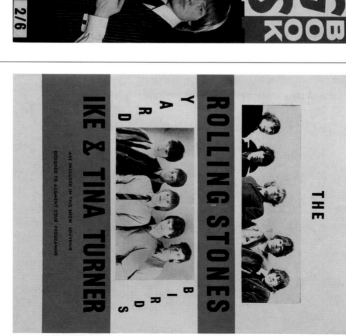

Original program supplement for a tour featuring The Rolling Stones and Ike and Tina Turner. ★☆☆☆☆

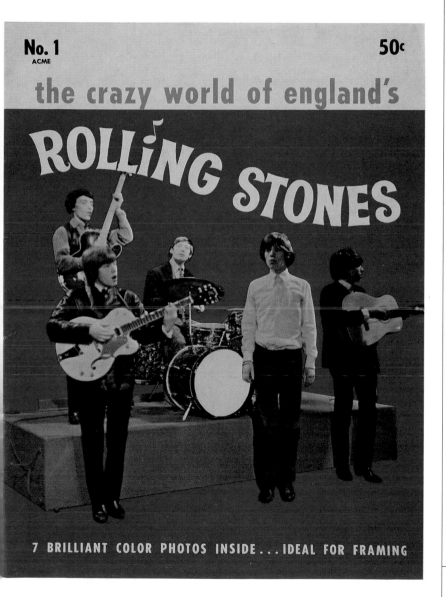

American "The Crazy World of England's Rolling Stones" souvenir program, Summer 1964, Issue No. 1. ★ ☆ ☆ ☆ ☆

Isle of Wight Festival weekend ticket.   *1969*   ★ ☆ ☆ ☆ ☆

REMEMBER THIS?

Bay City Rollers card and plastic lampshade.   ★☆☆☆☆

Cher, "All I Really Want To Do," stereo LP, SLBY 3058, released by Liberty. *1965* ★☆☆☆☆

p.224

p.358

p.338

p.145

p.366

p.113

p.344

p.322

p.357

p.333

p.181

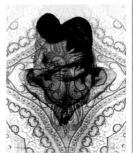

p.353

p.389

p.395

p.352

p.141

p.334

p.385

WHOLE LOTTA LOVE

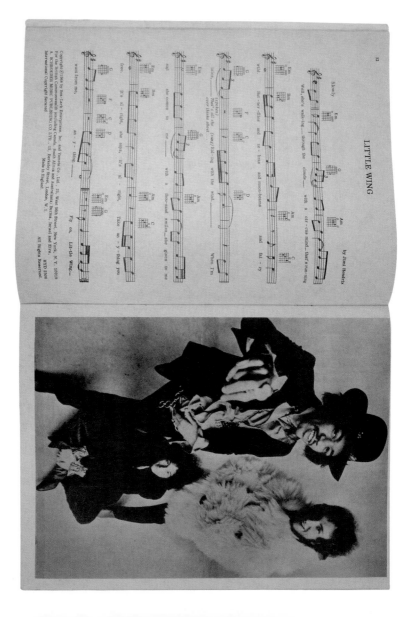

DETAIL: Page 12 of songbook, including lyrics and music for "Little Wing" and a photograph of Hendrix and band.

Jimi Hendrix Experience "Axis: Bold as Love" songbook, published by A. Schroeder Music Publishing Co. Ltd. *1968* ★☆☆☆☆

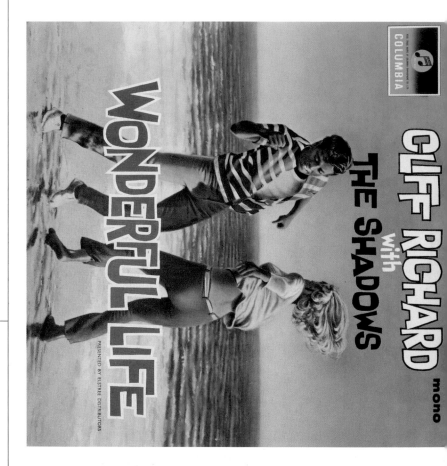

Cliff Richard with The Shadows "Wonderful Life" LP. ★☆☆☆☆

Cliff Richard and the Shadows "Finders Keepers" UK quad poster; framed and glazed. *c.1966* ★★☆☆☆

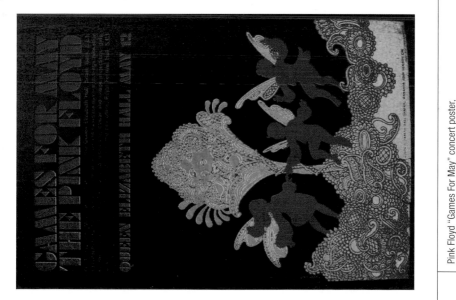

Pink Floyd "Games For May" concert poster, featuring three dancing silhouetted fairies, by Barry Zaid. *1967* ★★★★

Soundtrack of the James Bond film "From Russian with Love," from King Stereo, featuring the "Kiss-Theme" from Niagara on side B; 45rpm, BS-7019. 1963 ★☆☆☆☆

Bonanza "Ponderosa Ranch" lithographed tin mug; made in Hong Kong. ★ ☆☆☆

Dr. Who "The Mysterious Daleks" black battery-operated figure, by Marx Toys, with eyepiece and weapons. *1964* ★★ ☆☆

Italian poster for the Michelangelo Antonioni film "Blow-Up." ★★★☆☆

British quad poster for the film "Easy Rider." *1969* ★★★☆☆

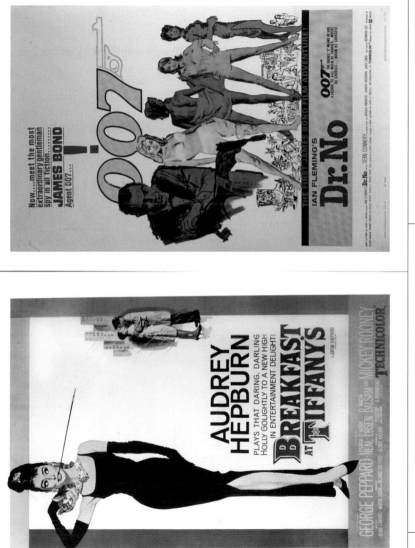

US one sheet linen-backed poster for the James Bond film "Dr. No." *1962* ★★★★

US three sheet poster, with iconic image of Audrey Hepburn, for the film "Breakfast At Tiffany's;" framed and glazed. *1961* ★★★★

Argentine poster for the film "Barbarella," starring Jane Fonda, with typical 1960s colorful artwork. *1968* ★★★★★

East German A1 poster for the film "My Fair Lady," with artwork by Westphal. *1967* ★ ★ ☆ ☆

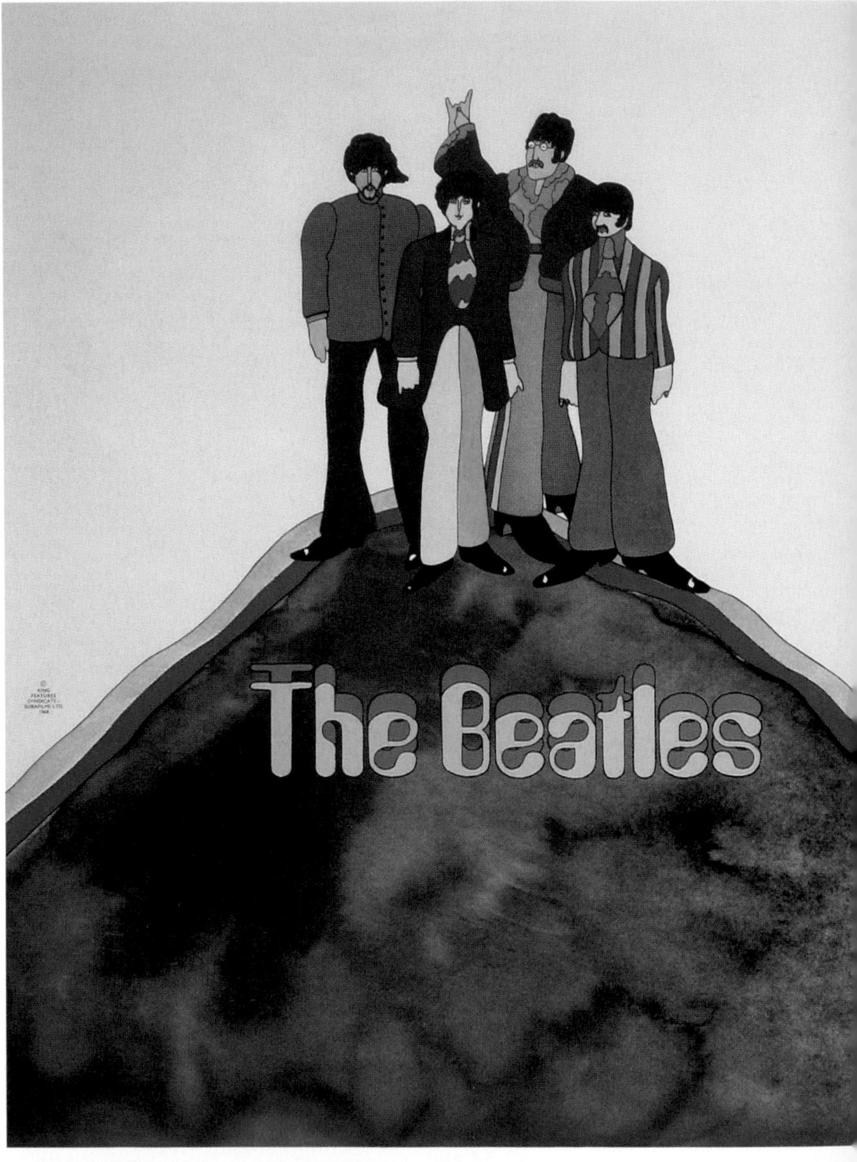
The Beatles

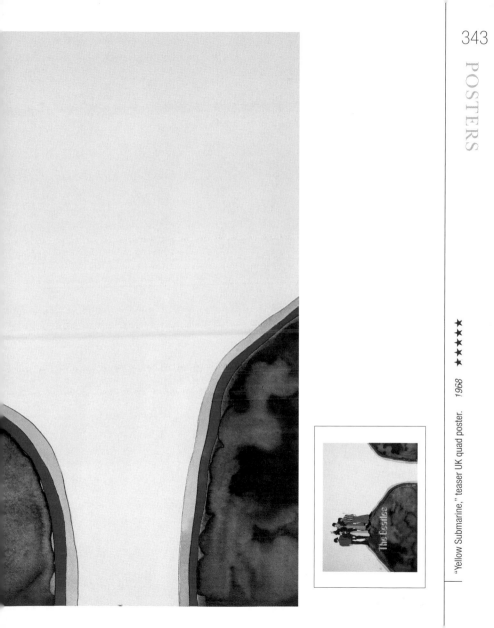

★★★★ 1968

"Yellow Submarine," teaser UK quad poster.

LOVE

The use of short words in large colorful letters is typical of Pop artist Robert Indiana's work. The "LOVE" poster is his most famous image. It was created for a Museum of Modern Art (MoMA) Christmas card in 1964, and then reused on a United States Postal Service (USPS) stamp in 1973. It also subsequently formed the basis of a sculpture in John F. Kennedy Plaza, Philadelphia.

Born in 1928 in Indiana as Robert Clark, Indiana studied at various art schools before settling in New York in 1954. Traffic signs, automatic amusement machines, and commercial stencils inspired his early works and in the early 1960s he developed his style of vivid color surfaces, involving letters, words, and numbers. Indiana became known for silkscreen prints, posters, and sculptures, which had as their theme the word LOVE. Robert Indiana has lived in Maine since 1978.

"LOVE" poster, designed by American artist Robert Indiana. ★★☆☆☆

"Are You Experienced," an American psychedelic poster.

★★☆☆☆

"Hair is beautiful," a Canadian psychedelic poster. ★★☆☆☆

Pietro Psaier "New York Rock Conexion Madrid," hand-colored poster of praying Jimi Hendrix with peacock feather decoration; mounted, framed, and glazed. ★★★★☆

REMEMBER THIS?

DETAIL: Marijuana leaves in the foreground.

This poster is based on Grant Wood's 1930 painting American Gothic.

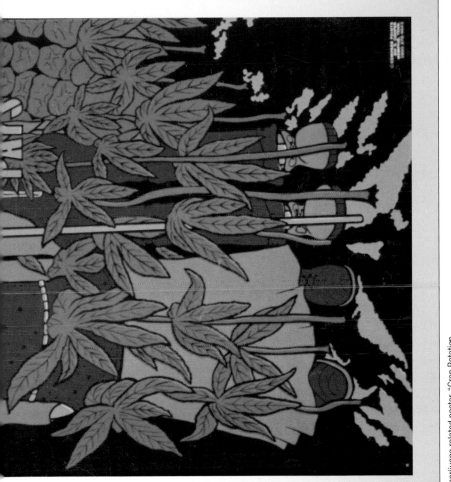

American marijuana related poster, "Crop Rotation Pays." It parodies the morally virtuous pastoral life in the American Midwest. ★★☆☆☆

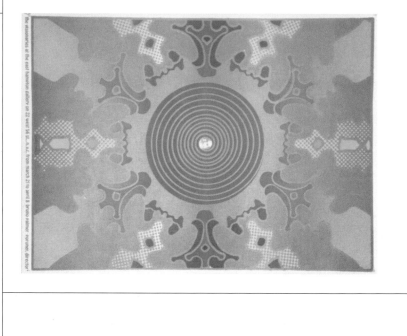

"Visionaries at the East Hampton Gallery," a Peter Max poster in psychedelic colors. ★★☆☆

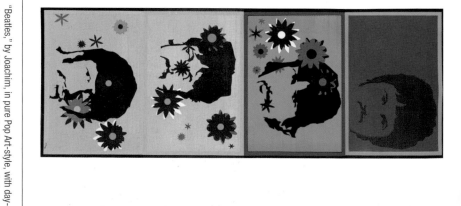

"Beatles," by Joachim, in pure Pop Art-style, with day-glo colors and flowers, celebrating the group during the "Flower Power" period. 1968 ★★★★☆

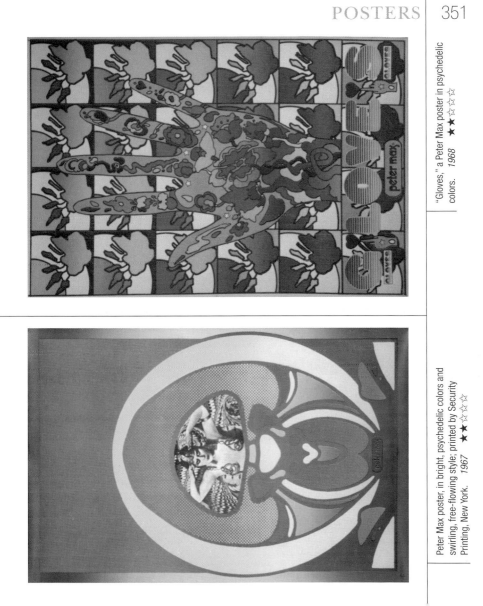

"Gloves," a Peter Max poster in psychedelic colors. *1968* ★ ★ ☆ ☆ ☆

Peter Max poster, in bright, psychedelic colors and swirling, free-flowing style; printed by Security Printing, New York. *1967* ★ ★ ☆ ☆ ☆

"Y-Front shorts put you in great shape" color photographic advertisement card standee. ★☆☆☆☆

"Make Love Not War" poster. ★★☆☆☆

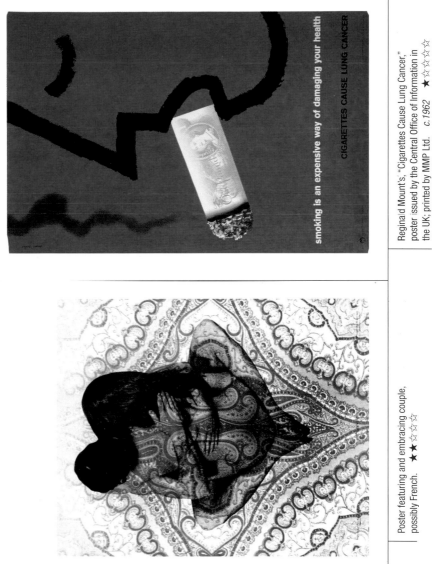

Reginald Mount's, "Cigarettes Cause Lung Cancer," poster issued by the Central Office of Information in the UK; printed by MMP Ltd. *c.1962* ★ ☆ ☆ ☆

smoking is an expensive way of damaging your health

CIGARETTES CAUSE LUNG CANCER

Poster featuring and embracing couple, possibly French. ★ ★ ☆ ☆

PLAYBOY

One of the world's best-known brands, the "Playboy" bunny's head has appeared on the cover of every Playboy magazine since the second issue released in early 1954. Playboy's founder Hugh Hefner chose a rabbit as the symbol for his magazine because "of the humorous sexual connotation, and because he offered an image that was frisky and playful." Art Paul, Playboy's first art director, sketched the bunny within half an hour.

The 1960s were Playboy's golden age, and by 1968 the magazine was selling five million copies. Many celebrities, from Marilyn Monroe to Madonna, have appeared on the cover and as "centerfolds" over the years. The company has since developed into Playboy Enterprises, reaching into every form of media. Playboy remains one of the leading men's magazines.

Gold-plated Playboy bunny pin. ★ ☆☆☆☆

Playboy bunny gold-plated bracelet, with the eye inset with a red diamanté. ★☆☆☆☆

Playboy Playmate "Complete Playboy Centerfold" puzzle, contained in a tin with paper label; has all pieces intact. *c.1968* ★★☆☆☆

Penthouse, vol. 1, no. 9, with "The Nudest Miss World" cover. ★ ☆☆☆

Playboy matchbook, from Phoenix. The Playboy Club in Phoenix, Arizona opened on December 19, 1962. ★☆☆☆

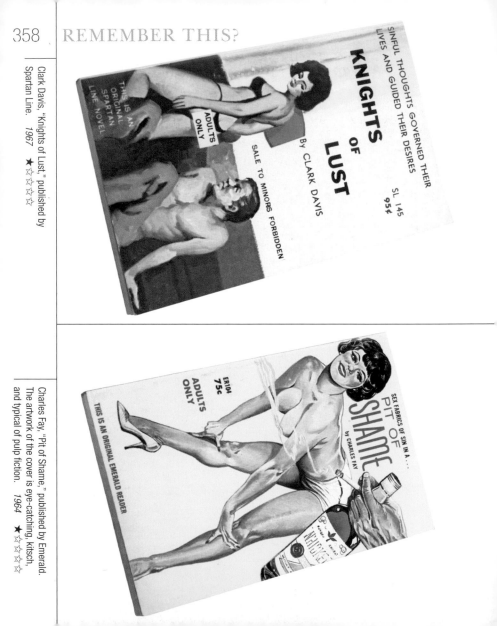

Clark Davis, "Knights of Lust," published by Spartan Line. *1967* ★☆☆☆☆

Charles Fay, "Pit of Shame," published by Emerald. The artwork of the cover is eye-catching, kitsch, and typical of pulp fiction. *1964* ★☆☆☆☆

THIS ARTICLE IS NOT:-
1. To be sold to a person under the age of 18 years.
2. To be demonstrated in public.
3. To be sold through the post as a mail-order item or to a person who has not first had an opportunity to inspect it fully.

4 style

sexy
drinking
straw

DETAIL: Embracing couple on the back of the box of "Sexy Drinking Straws."

Box of "Sexy Drinking Straws," made in Hong Kong. ★☆☆☆

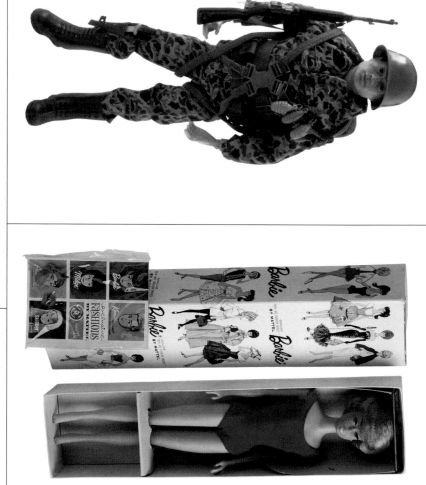

"Paratrooper – US" Action Man figure, by Palitoy. ★★☆☆☆

Platinum Bubble Barbie, with red swimsuit, red shoes and booklet; has original box. 1963 ★★☆☆☆

"Hair Fair" Barbie doll, in a psychedelic outfit. *1968* ★★☆☆☆

Brunette "Bubble Cut" Barbie doll, in a "Solo in Spotlight" outfit. *1962* ★★☆☆☆

"Beautiful Crissy" doll, by Ideal, with original dress, shoes, "Letter to Mother" care instructions, and box with early wool handle. *1969* ★ ☆☆☆☆

Mattel dressed Barbie No. 1, with complete accessories, including necklace, earrings, and purse; extremely rare. ★★★★★

BARBIE

With her hourglass figure, endless legs, and expansive closet of outfits, Barbie is the most popular fashion doll ever created and has become a true 20th-century icon. In 1959, Ruth and Eliot Handler, the founders of Mattel, introduced a fresh-faced doll with a high ponytail and black and white striped swimsuit at the American Toy Fair in New York City. The doll, which was named after the couple's daughter Barbara, received mixed reviews at first as she was unlike any doll seen before. However, by 1960 her popularity was assured.

In the 1960s, as today, Barbie had a succession of fashionable hairstyles and outfits — from chic "bubble-cut" hair to trendy bathing suits. From 1964, as teenagers adopted the "Carnaby Street" look, Barbie's dresses became shorter and her hair longer. In 1967, a new face was sculpted, which brought her up to date for the next generation of little girls.

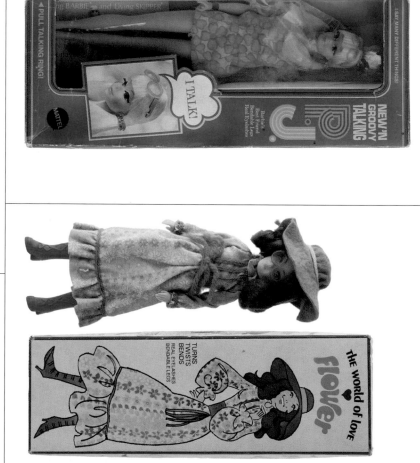

Talking P.J. doll, in original box. 1969 ★★★☆☆

Hasbro "The World of Love – Flower" doll, which turns, twists, and bends; has original box. ★★☆☆☆

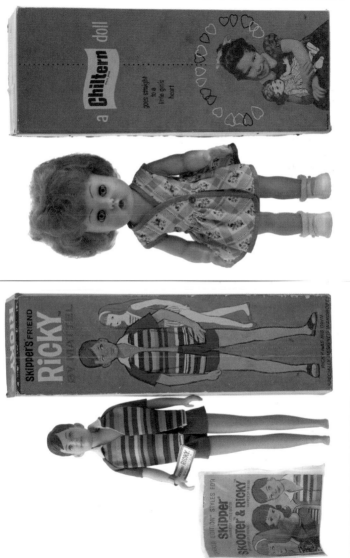

Chiltern vinyl girl doll, with tight curl "Saran" rough-textured hair; has original box. ★ ☆☆☆

Mattel Ricky doll, in original box. 1964 ★★☆☆

Hot Wheels® neon pink Classic 36 Ford Coupé, model 6253, by Mattel. *1969* ★★★☆☆

Hot Wheels® bronze Twinmill, model 6258,
by Mattel. *1968* ★ ☆ ☆ ☆

Corgi gift set No. 40 "The Avengers," with "John Steed's" red Bentley, with wire wheels, and "Emma Peel's" Lotus; has two figures, three umbrellas, and box lacking one end-flap. *1967* ★★★☆☆

Corgi No. 277 "The Monkees" Monkeemobile, in red, with white roof, and with cast wheels; has blue and yellow window box. *1968* ★★☆☆☆

SECRET OPERATING FEATURES

OPENING ROOF AND EJECTOR SEAT

REAR BULLET SCREEN

SPECIAL AGENT 007

JAME

ASTON MA

IN THE D

CORGI TOYS

SPECIAL AGENT 007©

JAMES BOND'S

ASTON MARTIN D.B.5

This model car is gold, with silver wire wheels and bumper, and a red interior.

Corgi No. 261 "James Bond" Aston Martin DB5, with secret instructions in opened packet and self-adhesive unused 007 badge. *1967* ★ ★ ☆ ☆ ☆

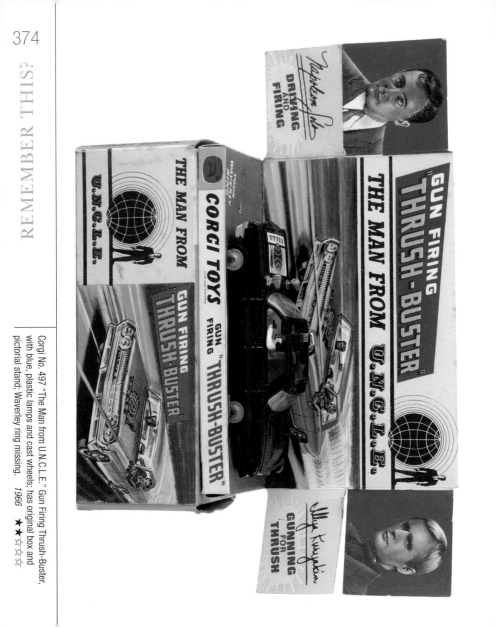

Corgi No. 497 "The Man from U.N.C.L.E." Gun Firing Thrush-Buster, with blue, plastic lamps and cast wheels; has original box and pictorial stand; Waverley ring missing. *1966* ★★☆☆☆

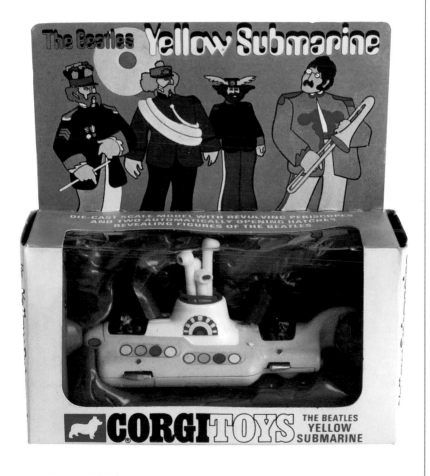

Corgi No. 803 "The Beatles" Yellow Submarine, with four periscopes, two red hatch covers, and four figures; has original box. ★★★☆☆

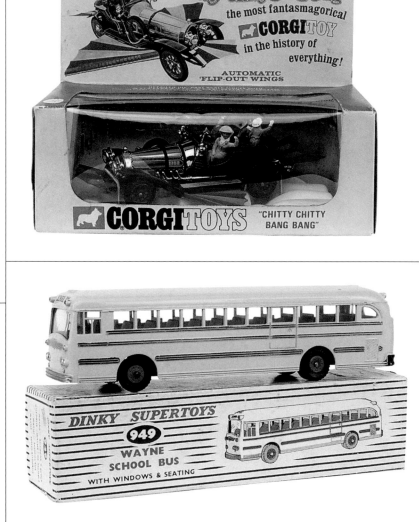

Corgi No. 266 "Chitty Chitty Bang Bang," with all four character figures, in original window box. *1968* ★★☆☆☆

Dinky No.949 Wayne School Bus, in yellow, with red interior, black side flashes, and red plastic hubs; has original box. ★★★☆☆

Dinky No. 100 "Thunderbirds" Lady Penelope's
FAB 1, including roof slides, missile, and
harpoons. *1968* ☆☆☆ ★★

Pelham Mickey Mouse puppet, with original box. *c.1960* ★★☆☆☆

Pelham "Wicked Witch" puppet, with tag, original control bar, and colored strings; has instruction sheet and original box. *1963* ★★ ☆☆☆

Pelham guitarist puppet, in purple pants and psychedelic top, similar in appearance to George Harrison, in original box marked "SL16 Guitarist." ★★ ☆☆☆

Japanese battery driven tin toy robot, made by Alps, with scenes from Mars on TV screen and rotating eyes. *1960* ★★★☆☆

"Lost In Space" battery powered robot,
manufactured by Remco Industries, marked
"© Space Productions."   c.1966   ★★★☆☆

BLAST FROM THE PAST

p.391

p.363

p.323

p.174

p.54

p.397

p.415

p.261

p.414

p.35

p.436

p.63

Rare "Doctor Who Give-A-Show Projector," by Chad Valley. *c.1965* ★★☆☆☆

DETAIL: Interior of box of "Doctor Who Give-A-Show Projector."

Hasbro "The Game of Love," dated and with original box. *1969* ★★☆☆☆

DETAIL: "The Game of Love" is comparable with the famous party game Twister.

"Twiggy" game, by MB Games. The object of the game is to cover Twiggy's face with matching cards. *1967* ★ ★ ☆ ☆

Waddingtons "Bonanza Michigan Rummy Game," reproduced with the permission of NBC. 1964 ★ ☆☆☆☆

"Dan Dare Planet Gun," by Merit, has orginal box. ★★☆☆☆

Plastic "Peace on Barrel" urinating toy. If the barrel is full, the man "urinates" when a button at the back is pushed; has original box. ★ ☆☆☆

Marusan tinplate "Smoky Joe" car with battery-operated "Mystery Action" of a man smoking a pipe. ★★☆☆☆

Slinky, by James Industries Inc., with original box. ★☆☆☆☆

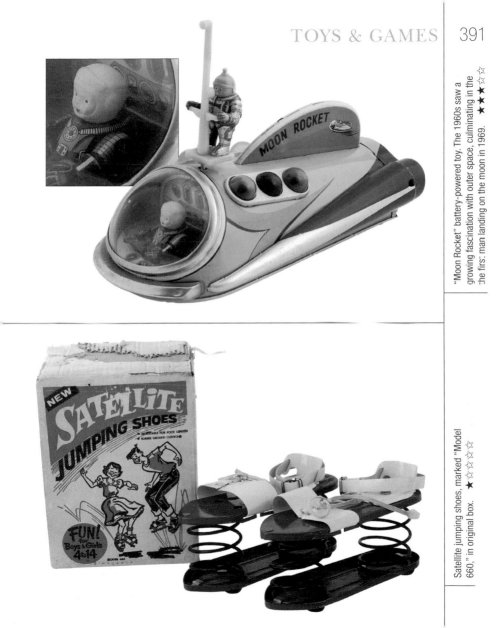

"Moon Rocket" battery-powered toy. The 1960s saw a growing fascination with outer space, culminating in the the firs: man landing on the moon in 1969. ★★★☆☆

Satellite jumping shoes, marked "Model 660," in original box. ★☆☆☆☆

Troll, by Thomas Dam, with green felt shorts; has original box. ★☆☆☆☆

"Astronaut" Action Man figure, with space capsule. ★★☆☆☆

Vinyl inflatable child doll, with bell inside, by Alvimar Corporation, for the New York World Fair 1964–65. ★ ☆☆☆☆

Paris "Hippie" figure, signed "Anna Love Melanie" on base. ★ ☆☆☆☆

"Mr Wupper" ceiling mounted, molded space creature, in plastic, by Wupper Design Ltd; has original box. ★★☆☆☆

"Kiddi-Tunes" 78rpm, battery-operated record player, by Marx Toys of Swansea; has original box. ★★☆☆☆

☆☆☆☆ ★

c. 1960

Acme Toys lithographed tin sand pail.

"Gay Day" giraffe, in psychedelic printed orange and pink fabric.
Made in South Africa. ★☆☆☆☆

Program for the 1966 World Cup 1966 final tie. ★☆☆☆☆

Daily Express guide to the 1966 World Cup final tie. ★☆☆☆☆

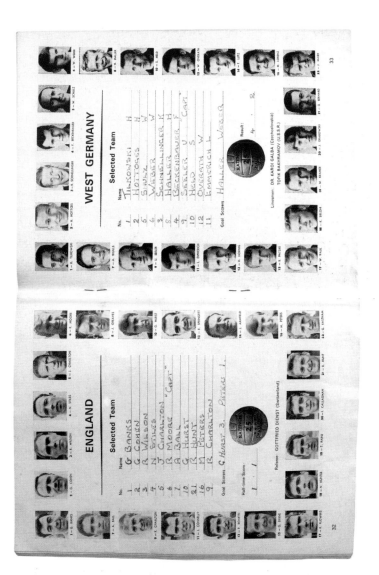

DETAIL: Pages from World Cup Final
1966 program shown left.

DETAIL: Pages from scrapbook on p.404. At the 1966 World Cup, Willie – a British lion wearing the Union Jack – became the first official mascot in the history of the competition.

© FOOTBALL ASSOCIATION 1963-1966
COLLINS/WORLD CUP COLLECTORS CLUB

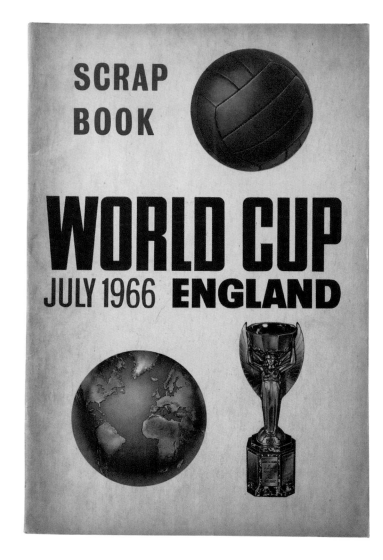

World Cup scrap book, printed for the Football
Association by Collins World Cup Collectors Club;
unused. *1996* ★★☆☆☆

Benfica v. Manchester United European Cup Final soccer program, May 29, 1968. United won 4–0: the first English team to win the European Cup. *1968* ★ ☆☆☆☆

George Best lamp, with original shade, plastic base, carved wood football, printed paper shade, and facsimile signature. ★★ ☆☆☆

Empty Ted Williams baseball card display box, by Fleer, with lid and side aprons, picturing a color portrait of Williams.   ★★★☆☆

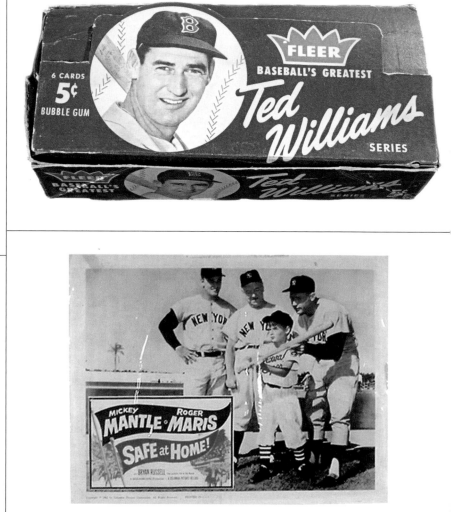

"Safe at Home" lobby card, featuring Mickey Mantle, Roger Maris, and Casey Stengel, depicting batting tips being given by the three Yankees stars.   *1962*   ★★☆☆☆

Dick Schaap, "Mickey Mantle - The Indispensable Yankee," first edition paperback, published by Bartholomew House, Inc.　*1961*　★ ☆☆☆☆

Rare New York National League Baseball Club official program and score card.　*1963*　★ ☆☆☆

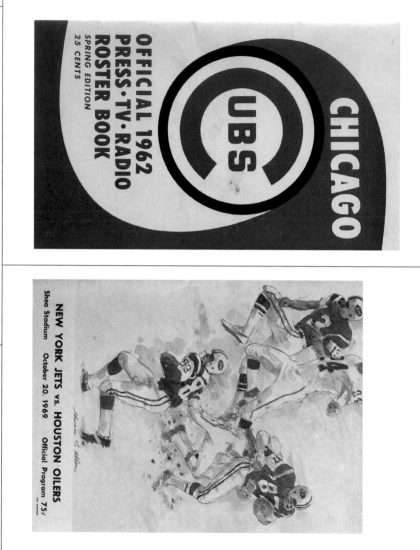

Chicago Cubs Official 1962 Roster Book. ★☆☆☆☆

New York Jets vs Houston Oilers, official program; held at Shea Stadium, Oct 20, 1969. ★☆☆☆☆

Ted Williams Camp gray flannel, youth-size, baseball shirt, signed on the front by Williams in black felt-tip pen. ★★☆☆☆

Aladdin Industries Peter Pan lunchbox and Thermos flask. *1969* ★★☆☆☆

Thermos Chitty Chitty Bang Bang lunchbox. Thermos flask is missing, affecting the value detrimentally. *1969* ★★☆☆☆

"Go Go" vinyl lunchbox (lacks Thermos), by Aladdin Incorporated; damaged. *c.1966* ★★☆☆☆

Aladdin Enterprises "Snoopy" dome-topped metal lunchbox and Thermos bottle. *c.1970* ★★☆☆☆

An Aladdin Jetsons dome-top lunchbox and Thermos flask. *1963* ★★★★★

Thermos MLB baseball lunchbox, with rare magnetic game still present, with counters, to play game on reverse, also with Thermos flask. *c.1968* ★ ☆☆☆

"Beatles Yellow Submarine" metal lunchbox and thermos. *1968* ★★★★☆

"The Pussycats" vinyl lunchbox and Thermos flask, by Aladdin Incorporated. The Thermos is covered with a paper label. *c.1966* ★ ★ ☆ ☆ ☆

Ohio Art "Flower Power" printed metal lunchbox. ★ ☆ ☆ ☆ ☆

PRIVATE FACES

TWIGGY, THE QUEEN, PRINCE PHILIP, THE POPE, FROST ETC...PAGE 60

TWIGGY

A stick-thin figure, boyish haircut, and striking eyelashes made Twiggy the face of the Swinging Sixties. Born as Lesley Hornby in London in 1949, she was discovered as a 15-year-old by the man who was to become her manager, Justin de Villeneuve. After being named "The Daily Express Face of 1966," Twiggy became the first "supermodel" and appeared on the front cover of many magazines. Her distinctive waif-like style was the exact opposite of the curvaceous pin-ups of the 1950s. Desperate to achieve the look, millions of girls around the globe dieted, pouted, and curled their eyelashes. Fans could even buy Twiggy clothing from 1967, but only if they could slip into the tiny sizes the outfits were produced in. As well as a successful modeling career, Twiggy has starred in film, stage, and television productions and recorded many albums. She continues to work in the entertainment industry today.

NOVA, October 1968, with Twiggy on the cover and a feature on Henry Ford. Nova was first published in 1965 and became the style bible for the 1960s in the UK. ★ ☆ ☆ ☆ ☆

LIFE
INTERNATIONAL

20 PAGES IN COLOR
STORYBOOK AFRICA
As great writers saw it

MARRIAGE—AND DIVORCE—IN AMERICA !

LIFE, October 23, 1961, international edition, with Elizabeth
Taylor as "Cleopatra" on the cover. ★☆☆☆

SPECIAL SECTION

LIFE

THE VIEW FROM THE MOON

IN COLOR: PICTURES FROM APOLLO VIII

The earth as seen
from Apollo VIII in space,
showing the outlines of
North and South America

2/6

Ireland inc. tax

JANUARY 20 · 1969

LIFE, January 20, 1969, with a picture of Earth as seen from the Apollo VIII spacecraft on the cover. ★☆☆☆

LIFE

MRS. KENNEDY,
CAROLINE
AND JOHN JR.
WAIT TO JOIN
PROCESSION
TO CAPITOL

DECEMBER 6 · 1963 · 25¢

LIFE, December 6, 1963, with a picture from John F. Kennedy's funeral on the cover. ★ ☆☆☆☆☆

QUEEN 2/-

OCTOBER 23rd 1962

JANE FONDA DREAMS OF
LOVE AND OTHER THINGS
Fashion: IF THE COAT
FITS, WEAR IT

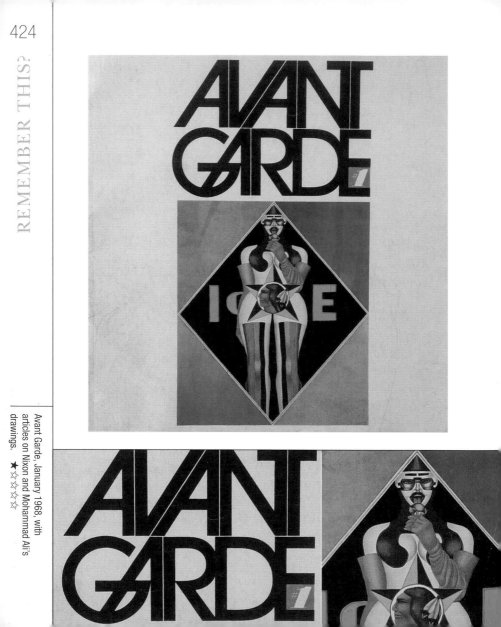

Avant Garde, January 1968, with articles on Nixon and Mohammad Ali's drawings. ★ ☆☆☆☆

Anthony Burgess "A Clockwork Orange," first edition, with first issue dustwrapper and original cloth binding; published by Heinemann, London. ★★★★☆

Ian Fleming, "You Only Live Twice," first edition, published by Jonathan Cape. *1964* ★★☆☆

smoking is an expensive way of damaging your health

p.353

p.315

p.432

p.325

p.420

p.401

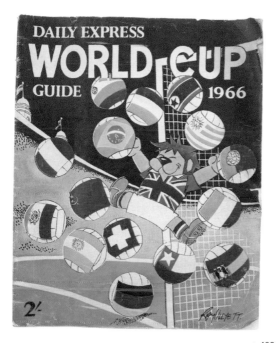

p.400

p.432

p.357

p.419

p.386

Santa Claus on green skis, plastic lolly holder. ★☆☆☆☆

Plastic Christmas clown and drum toy, with moving wheels. ★★☆☆☆

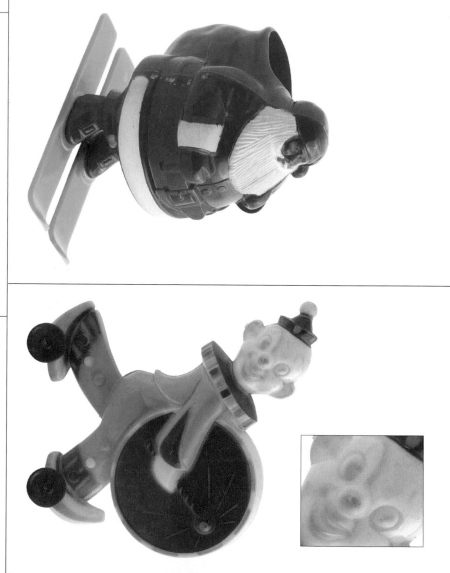

Halloween black and orange plastic
pumpkin lolly holder. ★ ☆☆☆☆

Mercury MA-8 Wally Schirra signed copy of "The Astronauts, Pioneers in Space," published by Golden Book Press and the editors of LIFE magazine. *1961* ★ ☆☆☆☆

Yuri Gagarin photograph, signed in purple ink along the upper left-hand edge of the piece. ★★★★☆

Spaceman Staffordshire Potteries mug, made to commemorate the moon landing. *c.1969* ★ ☆☆☆

Painted, cast iron money bank, with red "Apollo 8" capsule circling the "moon" on a blue base, marked "Borman, Lovell, Anders" on one side. ★ ☆☆☆

BORMAN LOVELL ANDERS

New York World's Fair, 1964, plastic money bank, with original box. *c.1961* ★ ☆☆☆☆

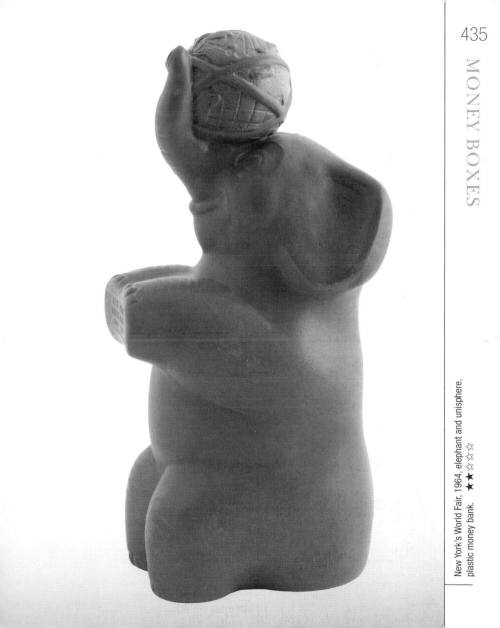

New York's World Fair, 1964, elephant and unisphere, plastic money bank. ★ ★ ☆☆☆

Carlton Ware snail money box, from the "bug-eye" series. *c.1965* ★☆☆☆☆

"Piggly Wiggly" stores advertising money box in plastic. ★☆☆☆☆

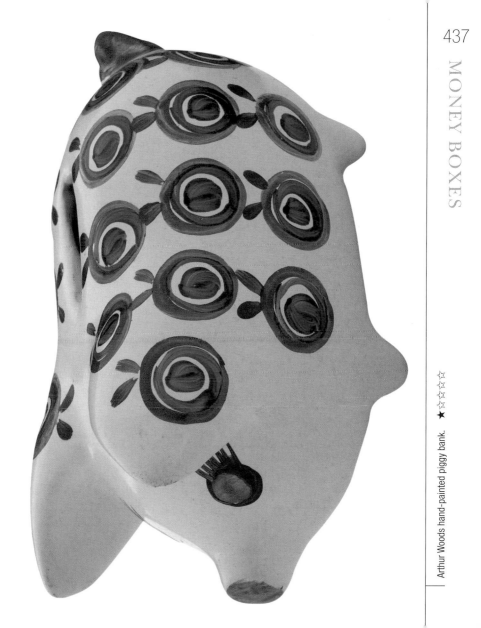

★ ☆☆☆☆ | Arthur Woods hand-painted piggy bank.

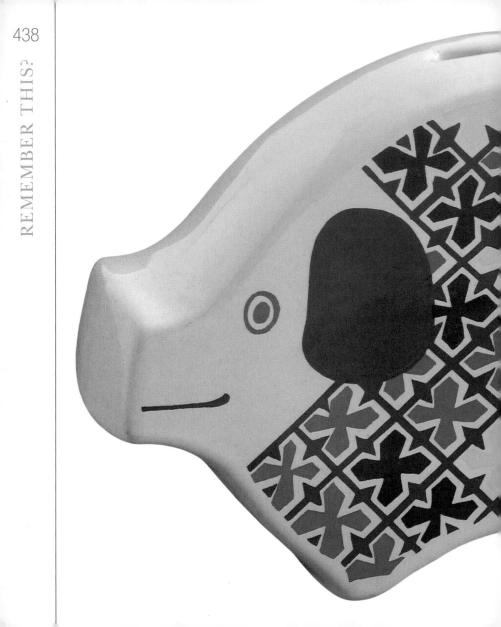

MONEY BOXES

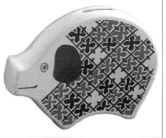

☆☆☆☆ ★

Carlton Ware "Flatback" series psychedelic piggy money box, designed by Vivienne Brennan.

USING THE INTERNET

★ The internet has revolutionized the trading of collectibles as it provides a cost-effective way of buying and selling, away from the overheads of shops and auction rooms. Many millions of collectibles are offered for sale and traded daily, with sites varying from global online marketplaces, such as eBay, to specialist dealers' websites.

★ When searching online, remember that some people may not know how to accurately describe their item. General category searches, even though more time consuming, and even purposefully misspelling a name, can yield results. Also, if something looks too good to be true, it probably is. Using this book to get to know your market visually, so that you can tell the difference between a real bargain and something that sounds like one, is a good start.

★ As you will understand from buying this book, color photography is vital – look for online listings that include as many images as possible and check them carefully. Beware that colors can appear differently, even between computer screens.

★ Always ask the vendor questions about the object, particularly regarding condition. If there is no image, or you want to see another aspect of the object – ask. Most sellers (private or trade) will want to realize the best price for their items so will be more than happy to help – if approached politely and sensibly.

★ As well as the "e-hammer" price, you will probably have to pay additional transactional fees such as packing, shipping, and possibly regional or national taxes. It is always best to ask for an estimate of these additional costs before leaving a bid. This will also help you tailor your bid as you will have an idea of the maximum price the item will cost if you are successful.

★ As well as the well-known online auction sites, such as eBay, there is a host of other online resources for buying and selling, for example fair and auction date listings.

DEALERS AND AUCTION HOUSES

Adrian Grater
Georgian Village, Camden
Passage, London N1
Tel: 0208 579 0357
adriangrater@tiscali.co.uk

Andrea Hall Levy
PO Box 1243, Riverdale,
NY 10471 USA
Tel: 001 646 441 1726
barangrill@aol.com

Art Deco Etc
73 Upper Gloucester Road,
Brighton, Sussex BN1 3LQ
Tel: 01273 329 268
johnclark@artdecoetc.co.uk

Artius Glass
Street, Somerset BA16 0AN
Tel: 01458 443 694
www.artiusglass.co.uk

At The Movies
17 Fouberts Place,
London W1F 7QD
Tel: 020 7439 6336
www.atthemovies.co.uk

Atomic Age
318 East Virginia Road,
Fullerton, CA 92831, USA
Tel: 001 714 446 0736
atomage100@aol.com

Auction Team Köln
Postfach 50 11 19,
Bonnerstrasse 528-530, D-
50971 Cologne, Germany
Tel: 00 49 221 38 70 49
www.breker.com

Aurora Bijoux
Tel: 001 215 872 7808
www.aurorabijoux.com

**Aurora Galleries
International**
30 Hackamore Lane, Suite 2,
Bell Canyon, CA 91307 USA
Tel: 001 818 884 6468
www.auroragalleriesonline.com

Barbara Blau
South Street Antiques
Market 615 South 6th Street,
Philadelphia, PA 19147 USA
Tel: 001 215 739 4995
bbjools@msn.com

Bébés et Jouets
c/o Lochend Post Office,
165 Restalrig Road,
Edinburgh EH7 6HW
Tel: 0131 332 5650
bebesjouets@tiscali.co.uk

Beverley
30 Church Street,
London NW8 8EP
Tel: 020 7262 1576
www.alfiesantiques.com

Beyond Retro
110–112 Cheshire Street,
London E2 6EJ
Tel: 020 7613 3636
www.beyondretro.com

Biblion
1–7 Davies Mews, London
W1K 5AB
Tel: 020 7629 1374
www.biblion.com

**Black Horse
Antique Showcase**
2222 North Reading Road,
Denver PA, 17517 USA
Tel: 001 717 335 3300
www.antiques-showcase.com

Blanchard Ltd.
86/88 Pimlico Road,
London SW1W 8PL
Tel: 020 7823 6310

Bonhams Bond Sreet
101 New Bond Street,
London W1S 1SR
Tel: 020 7629 6602
www.bonhams.com

Bonhams Edinburgh
62 George Street,
Edinburgh EH2 2JL
Tel: 0131 225 2266
www.bonhams.com

British Doll Showcase
www.britishdollshowcase.
co.uk

Bukowskis
Arsenalsgatan 4, Box 1754,
111 87 Stockholm, Sweden
Tel: 00 46 8 614 08 00
www.bukowskis.se

**Cad Van Swankster at
The Girl Can't Help It**
Alfies Antiques Market, 13–25
Church Street, Marylebone,
London NW8 8DT
cad@sparklemoore.com

Cheffins
Clifton House, 1&2
Clifton Road, Cambridge,
Cambridgeshire CB1 7EA
Tel: 01223 213 343
www.cheffins.co.uk

China Search
P.O. Box 1202, Kenilworth,
Warwickshire CV8 2WW
Tel: 01926 512 402
www.chinasearch.co.uk

Chisholm Larsson
45 8th Avenue, New York
NY 10011 USA
Tel: 001 212 741 1703
www.chisholm-poster.com

Christine Wildman
wild123@allstream.net

Cloud Cuckoo Land
6 Charlton Place, Camden
Passage, London N1
Tel: 020 7354 3141

Cooper Owen
74 High Street, Egham,
Surrey TW20 9LF
Tel: 01784 434900
www.cooperowen.com

Cottees
The Market, East Street,
Wareham, Dorset BH20 4NR
Tel: 01929 552 826
www.auctionsatcottees.co.uk

The Country Seat
Huntercombe Manor Barn,
Nr Henley on Thames,
Oxon RG9 5RY
Tel: 01491 641349
www.whitefriarsglass.com

Cristobal
26 Church Street,
London NW8 8EP
Tel: 020 7724 7230
www.cristobal.co.uk

David Rago Auctions
333 North Main Street,
Lambertville, NJ 08530 USA
Tel: 001 609 397 9374
www.ragoarts.com

Design20C
Tel: 07946 0921 38
www.design20c.com

The Doll Express
No longer trading

Dorotheum
Palais Dorotheum, A-1010
Vienna, Dorotheergasse 17,
Austria
Tel: 0043 1 515 600
www.dorotheum.com

Dreweatt Neate Donnington Priory Salerooms
Donnington, Newbury,
Berkshire RG14 2JE
Tel: 01635 553 553
www.dnfa.com/donnington

Dreweatt Neate Godalming
Baverstock House,
93 High Street, Godalming,
Surrey GU7 1AL
Tel: 01483 423567
www.dnfa.com/godalming

The End of History
548 1/2 Hudson Street,
New York, NY 10014 USA
Tel: 001 212 647 7598

Emma Wilson Collection
Tel: 07989 493 831

Esther Harris, Vintage Eyewear of New York, USA
Tel: 001 646 319 9222

Festival
136 South Ealing Road,
London W5 3QJ
Tel: 020 8840 9333

Fragile Design
14/15 The Custard Factory,
Digbeth,
Birmingham B9 4AA
Tel: 0121 693 1001
www.fragiledesign.com

Fraser's Autographs
399 Strand,
London WC2R 0LX
Tel: 020 7836 9325
www.frasersautographs.com

Frederic Lozada Expertises
10 rue de Pomereu,
75116 Paris, France

Tel: 0033 153 70 98 90
www.fredericlozada.com

Freeman's
1808 Chestnut Street,
Philadelphia, PA 19103 USA
Tel: 001 215 563 9275
www.freemansauction.com

Gary Grant Choice Pieces
18 Arlington Way,
London EC1R 1UY
Tel: 020 7713 1122

Gentry Antiques
Gray's-in-the-Mews,
1–7 Davies Mews,
London W1K 5LP
Tel: 01993 832 252
www.cornishwarecollector.
co.uk

Geoffrey Robinson
Alfies Antiques Market,
13–25 Church Street,
London, NW8 8DT
Tel: 020 7723 0449
www.alfiesantiques.com

The Glass Merchant
Tel: 07775 683 961
as@titan98.freeserve.co.uk

Graham Cooley Collection
Mob: 07968 722 269
graham.cooley@metalysis.
com

Guernsey's Auctions
103 East 73rd Street, New
York, NY 10021, USA
Tel: 001 212 794 2280
www.guernseys.com

Herr Auctions
WG Herr Art & Auction House,
Friesenwall 35, 50672
Cologne, Germany
Tel: 0049 221 25 45 48
www.herr-auktion.de

Hilary Proctor
Advintage, Grays Antique
Market, 1–7 Davies Mews,
London W1Y 2PL
Tel: 020 7499 700
www.advintage.com

Holiday Happening
Private collection

Hunt Auctions
75 East Ulwchlan Avenue,
Suite 130, Exton,
PA 19341 USA
Tel: 001 610 524 0822
www.huntauctions.com

Huxtins
www.huxtins.com

Ingram Antiques
669 Mount Pleasant Road,
Toronto, Ontario
M4S 2N2, Canada
Tel: 001 416 484 4601

**Jeanette Hayhurst
Fine Glass**
32A Kensington Church
Street, London W8 4HA
Tel: 020 7938 1539

John Nicholsons
The Auction Rooms,
"Longfield," Midhurst Road,
Fernhurst, Haslemere,
Surrey GU27 3HA
Tel: 01428 653 727
www.johnnicholsons.com

Junkyard Jeweler
www.junkyardjeweler.com

Kathy's Korner
Tel: 001 516 624 9494

Keller & Ross
PO Box 783, Melrose,
MA 02716, USA
Tel: 001 978 988 2070
kellerross@aol.com

Larry & Dianna Elman
PO Box 415, Woodland Hills,
CA 91365, USA

Linda Bee
Grays Antique Market,
58 Davies Street,
London W1Y 2LP
Tel: 020 7629 5921
www.graysantiques.com

Lost City Arts
18 Cooper Square, New York,
NY 10003, USA
Tel: 001 212 375 0500
www.lostcityarts.com

Luna
23 George Street,
Nottingham NG1 3BH
Tel: 0115 924 3267
www.luna-online.co.uk

Lyon and Turnbull Ltd.
33 Broughton Place,
Edinburgh EH1 3RR
Tel: 0131 557 8844
www.lyonandturnbull.com

Manic Attic
Alfies Antiques Market, 13
Church Street,
London NW8 8DT
Tel: 020 7723 6105
manicattic@alfies.clara.net

Mark Hill Collection
Mob: 07798 915 474
stylophile@btopenworld.com

Mark Slavinsky
Private collection

Memory Lane
40–45 Bell Boulevard, Suite
109, Bayside, NY 11361, USA
Tel: 001 718 428 8181
memlnny@aol.com

Mick Collins
174 Portsmouth Road,
Horndean, Waterlooville,
Hampshire PO8 9HP
admin@sylvaclub.com

Million Dollar Babies
Tel: 001 518 885 7397

Mix Gallery
17 South Main Street,
Lambertville, NJ 08530, USA
Tel: 001 609 773 0777
www.mix-gallery.com

Mod-Girl
South Street Antiques
Center, 615 South 6th Street,
Philadelphia, PA 19147 USA
Tel: 001 215 592 0256

Mullock Madeley
The Old Shippon, Wall-under-
Heywood, Church Stretton,
Shropshire SY6 7DS
Tel: 0169 477 1771
www.mullockmadeley.co.uk

The Multicoloured Time Slip
Unit S002, Alfies Antiques
Market, 13–25 Church Street,
London NW8 8DT
Mob: 07971 410 563
dave_a_cameron@hotmail.
com

Mum Had That
www.mumhadthat.com

Neet-O-Rama
93 West Main Street,
Somerville, NJ 08876 USA
Tel: 001 908 722 4600
www.neetstuff.com

Nick Batt Collection
Tel: 020 8455 0719

No Pink Carpet
Tel: 01785 249 802
www.nopinkcarpct.com

Onslows
The Coach House,
Manor Road, Stourpaine,
Dorset DT11 8TQ
Tel: 01258 488 838
www.onslows.co.uk

Paola & Iaia
Alfies Antiques Market,
13-25 Church Street,
London NW8 8DT
Tel: 07751 084 135
paolaeiaialondon@hotmail.
com

Phil Arthurhultz
PO Box 12336, Lansing,
MI 48901, USA
Tel: 001 517 334 5000

Posteritati
239 Center Street, New York,
NY 10013, USA
Tel: 001 212 226 2207
www.posteritati.com

**Quittenbaum
Kunstauktionen**
Hohenstaufenstraße 1,
D-80801, Munich, Germany
Tel: 00 49 89 33 00 75 6
www.quittenbaum.de

R20th Century
82 Franklin Street,
New York, NY 10013, USA
Tel: 001 212 343 7979
www.r20thcentury.com

Richard Ball Lighters
richard-ball@msn.com

Richard Wallis Antiks
Tel: 020 8529 1749
www.richardwallisantiks.com

Seaside Toy Center
Joseph Soucy
179 Main St, Westerly,
RI 02891 USA
Tel: 001 401 596 0962

Sign of the Tymes
Mill Antiques Center,
12 Morris Farm Road,
Lafayette, NJ 07848 USA
Tel: 001 973 383 6028
www.millantiques.com

The Silver Fund
1 Duke of York Street,
London SW1Y 6JP
Tel: 0207 839 7664
www.thesilverfund.com

Skinner, Inc.
The Heritage on the Garden,
63 Park Plaza, Boston,
MA 02116 USA
Tel: 001 617 350 5400
also at:
357 Main Street, Bolton,
MA 01740, USA
Tel: 001 978 7796 241
www.skinnerinc.com

**Sollo:Rago
Modern Auctions**
333 North Main Street,
Lambertville,
NJ 08530 USA
Tel: 001 609 397 9374
www.ragoarts.com

**Sparkle Moore at
The Girl Can't Help It**
Alfies Antiques Market, 13–25
Church Street, Marylebone,
London NW8 8DT
Tel: 020 7724 8984
www.sparklemoore.com

Steinberg & Tolkien
193 Kings Road,
London SW3 5ED
Tel: 020 7376 3660

Sue Mautner
No longer trading

**Swann Galleries
Image Library**
104 East 25th Street, New
York, NY 10010 USA
Tel: 001 212 254 4710
www.swanngalleries.com

Thos. Wm. Gaze & Son
Diss Auction Rooms. Roydon
Road, Diss, Norfolk IP22 4LN
Tel: 01379 650 306
www.twgaze.com

Twentieth Century Marks
Whitegates, Rectory Road,
Little Burstead, Nr Billericay,
Essex CM12 9TR
Tel: 01268 411 000
www.20thcenturymarks.co.uk

Toy Heroes
42 Westway, Caterham-on-
the-Hill, Surrey CR3 5TP
Tel: 0188 334 8001
www.toyheroes.co.uk

Vectis Auctions Ltd
Fleck Way, Thornaby,
Stockton on Tees TS17 9JZ
Tel: 01642 750 616
www.vectis.co.uk

VinMagCo
39/43 Brewer Street,
London W1R 9UD
Tel: 020 7439 8525
www.vinmag.com

Vintage Modes
Grays Antique Market,
1–7 Davies Mews,
London W1K 5LP
Tel: 020 7629 7034
www.vintagemodes.co.uk

Von Zezschwitz
Friedrichstrasse 1a,
80801 Munich, Germany
Tel: 0049 89 389 8930
www.von-zezschwitz.de

Wallis and Wallis
West Street Auction Galleries,
Lewes, East Sussex BN7 2NJ
Tel: 01273 480 208
www.wallisandwallis.co.uk

William Wain at Antiquarius
Antiquarius, 135 King's Road,
London SW3 4PW
Tel: 020 7351 4905
w.wain@btopenworld.com

Wiener Kunst Auktion
Palais Kinsky, Freyung 4,
1010 Vienna, Austria
Tel: 0043 1532 4200
www.palais-kinsky.com

Woolley and Wallis
51–61 Castle Street,
Salisbury, Wiltshire SP13SU
Tel: 01722 424 500
www.woolleyandwallis.co.uk

Zanotta
Via Vittorio Veneto 57,
20054 Nova Milanese, Italy
Tel: 0039 0362 4981
www.zanotta.it

INDEX

PICTURE CREDITS

The following images, photographed with permission from the sources itemized below
are copyright © Judith Miller and Dorling Kindersley.

Adrian Grater p.41, p.65, p.69; Andrea Hall Levy p.293, p.93; Art Deco Etc p.132; **Artius Glass** p.98; **Atomic Age** p.360, p.365 **At The Movies** p.339; **Auction Team Köln** p.236, p. 380; **Aurora Bijoux** p.285; **Aurora Galleries Int.** p.432, p.433; **Barbara Blau** p.276, p.281, p.283; **Bébés et Jouets** p.378; **Beverley** p.63; **Beyond Retro** p.273; **Biblion** p.426; **Black Horse** p.54, p.63, p.337, p.407, p.408; **Bonhams Edinburgh** p.205; **Donhams Bond St** p.196, p.221, p.225; **British Doll Showcase** p.43, p.367; **Bukowskis** p.190, p.213, p.217, p.218, p.249; **Cad Van Swankster** p.138, p.323, p.336, p.356, p.358; **Cheffins** p.370, p.374, p.377; **China Search** p.17, p.30, p.34, p.42; **Chisholm Larsson** p.338, p.345, p.346, p.348, p.350, p.351; **Christine Wildman** p.143, p.145; **Cloud Cuckoo Land** p.265; **Cooper Owen** p.317, p.318, p.321, p.323, p.335, p.347, p.379; **Cottees** p.36, p.37, p.38, p.40; **The Country Seat** p.122, p.81, p.94; **Cristobal** p.278, p.280, p.282, p.283, p.284; **David Rago Auctions** p.215, p.219, p.220, p.246, p.248; **Design20C** p.16, p.25, p.159, p.245, p.285, p.357; **The Doll Express** p.366;

Dorotheum p.149, p.218, p.224, p.227, p.228, p.243, p.247; **Dreweatt Neate** p.90, p.379; **Esther Harris Vintage Eyewear of New York** p.302, p.303, p.304, p.305, p.302, p.303, p.306; **The End of History** p.77, p.102, p.103, p.104, p.105, p.128, p.129; **Emma Wilson** p.112, p.114, p.115; **Festival** p.10, p.16, p.21, p.23, p.25, p.27, p.33, p.34, p.64; **Fragile Design** p.42, p.67, p.78, p.79, p.95, p.149, p.151, p.179, p.242, p.436, p.439; **Fraser's Autographs** p.432; **Frederic Lozada Expertises** p.347, p.352, p.353; **Freeman's** p.178, p.197, p.202, p.231, p.237, p.247, p.257; **Gentry** p.66; **Graham Cooley** p.62, p.88, p.91, p.109, p.117, p.127, p.132, p.133; **Gary Grant** p.18, p.19, p.20, p.28, p.32; **Geoffrey Robinson** p.12, p.13, p.137; **Guernsey's** p.326; **Herr Auctions** p.116, p.204, p.210, p.238, p.242; **Hilary Proctor** p.253; **Holiday Happenings** p.430, p.431; **Hunt** p.406, p.409, p.410; **Huxtins** p.165, p.309, p.391, p.397; **Ingram** p.101; **Jeanette Hayhurst** p.90, p.94, p.99; **John Nicholsons** p.197, p.200, p.209; **Junkyard Jeweler** p.281; **Keller & Ross** p.46, p.47, p.48, p.49; **Kathy's Korner** p.52; **Larry & Dianna**

Elman p.336; **Linda Bee** p.277, p.284, p.291; **Luna** p.45, p.68, p.72, p.137, p.155, p.157, p.160, p.163; **Lyon and Turnbull** p.207, p.228, 425; **Lost City Arts** p.206, p.215; **Manic Attic** p.110, p.111, p.142, p.175, p.239, p.352, p.396; **Mark Hill** p.89; **Mark Slavinksy** p.404; **Memory Lane** p.363, p.393, p.434; **Mick Collins** p.51, p.52, p.53; **Million Dollar Babies** p.276; **Mix Gallery** p.287, p.288, p.290, p.292, p.296, p.297, p.298; **Mod Girl** p.263; **Mullock Madeley** p.400; **The Multicoloured Time Slip** p.10, p.11, p.13, p.15, p.24, p.35, p.59, p.60, p.61, p.65, p.135, p.136, p.138, p.140, p.144, p.160, p.161, p.162, p.164, p.166, p.169, p.170, p.171, p.172, p.173, p.174, p.181, p.182, p.183, p.307, p.310, p.328, p.359, p.362, p.385, p.388, p.396, p.399, p.401, p.433, p.437; **Mum Had That** p.12, p.76, p.93, p.93, p.121, p.123; **Neet-O-Rama** p.113, p.115, p.141, p.145, p.150, p.167, p.174, p.252, p.254, p.255, p.258, p.259, p.260, p.261, p.267, p.268, p.271, p.272, p.294, p.295, p.299, p.327, p.353, p.361, p.366, p.367, p.368, p.381, p.389, p.391, p.395, p.411, p.415, p.424; **Nick Batt** p.360, p.392; **No Pink Carpet** p.70, p.73, p.86, p.87; **Onslows** p.352; **Paola & Iaia** p.356; **Phil Arthurhultz** p.435,

p.436; **Posteritati** p.338, p.340, p.341, p.342; **Private collection** p.404; **Quittenbaum** p.189, p.191, p.192, p.210, p.216, p.220, p.229, p.237, p.238, p.240, p.246; **R20th Century** p.193, p.235; **Richard Ball** p.148; **Richard Wallis** p.79, p.108; **Seaside Toy Center** p.410, p.411, p.412, p.413, p.414; **Sign of the Tymes** p.55, p.369, p.390, p.392, p.430; **Silver Fund** p.278; **Skinner, Inc.** p.203; **Sollo:Rago** p.196, p.211, p.217; **Sparkle Moore** p.50, p.267, p.268; **Steinberg & Tolkien** p.258, p.262, p.266, p.269; **Sue Mautner** p.279; **Swan Galleries** p.350; **Thos. Wm. Gaze & Son** p.44, p.134, p.39, p.148, p.151, p.152, p.194, p.214, p.221, p.243, p.248, p.249, p.316, p.318, p.319, p.320, p.322, p.324, p.325, p.326, p.329, p.333, p.334, p.336, p.337, p.388; **Toy Heroes** p.384, p.427; **Twentieth Century Marks** p.17, p.31, p.58, p.68, p.153; **VinMagCo** p.41/, p.419, p.420, p.421, p.422, p.423; **Vectis** p.371, p.376; **Vintage Sports Collection** p.357, p.407, p.408; **Von Zezschwitz** p.80, p.81, p.82, p.83, p.92, p.116, p.122; **Wallis and Wallis** p.373, p.375, p.390; **Weiner Kunst Auktion** p.150, p.188, p.195, p.223; **William Wain** p.279; **Woolley and Wallis** p.39, p.44, p.45; **Zanotta** p.230

ARCHIVE PICTURE ACKNOWLEDGMENTS

The publisher would like to thank the following for their kind permission to reproduce their material.

pp.8–9: **The Advertising Archives;** pp.74–75:**The Advertising Archives;** pp.130–31:**Getty Images/The image Bank/Archive Holdings Inc;** pp.186–87:**Adelta International/ Eero Aarnio;** pp.250–251: **Corbis/ Condé Nast Archive;** pp.312–13: **Rex Features/David Magnus.**

All other images © Dorling Kindersley and The Price Guide Company Ltd.

For further information see: www.dkimages.com

All jacket images © Dorling Kindersley and The Price Guide Company Ltd.

ACKNOWLEDGMENTS

AUTHOR'S ACKNOWLEDGMENTS

The Price Guide Company would like to thank the following for their contribution to the production of this book:

Photographer Graham Rae for his wonderful photography.

All of the dealers, auction houses, and private collectors for kindly allowing us to photograph their collections, especially David Cameron and Vincent Charlton at The Multicoloured Timeslip, Ian Broughton, Graham Cooley, Sparkle Moore at The Girl Can't Help it, The End of History, Fragile Design, and Neet-O-Rama.

Also special thanks to Mark Hill, Jessica Bishop, Dan Dunlavey, Julie Brooke, Cathy Marriott, Claire Smith, and Sara Sturgess for their editorial contribution and help with image sourcing.

Thanks also to Digital Image Co-ordinator Ellen Sinclair and Workflow Consultant Bob Bousfield.

PUBLISHER'S ACKNOWLEDGMENTS

Dorling Kindersley would like to thank the following for their contribution to the production of this book:

Sarah Smithies for picture research, Sara Sha'ath for proofreading, Tamsin Curtis for proofreading and co-ordinating proofs, Dawn Henderson and Kathryn Wilkinson for additional editorial help, and Hilary Bird for indexing.

MANUFACTURER'S NOTE